Big God

A New Believer's Guide To God

Big God Getting To Know Him
Book 1

Donna Ladner Bass

3 TREES

BIG GOD Getting To Know Him

Big God Series Book 1

Copyright ©2022 by Donna L Bass

3 Trees Publishing, 18024 Dedeaux Clan Road, Gulfport, MS 39503

3treespublishing@gmail.com

ISBN: 979-8-9860289-6-5 print

ISBN: 979-8-9860289-7-2 ebook

LCCN: 2022907588

Cover Design: Amy Rylander Art, amyrylanderarts@gmail.com

Bible Bibliography

NKJV: Scripture taken from the New King James Version®. Copyright © 1982 by Thomas Nelson. Used by permission. All rights reserved.

NIV: Scriptures taken from the Holy Bible, New International Version®, NIV®. Copyright © 1973, 1978, 1984, 2011 by Biblica, Inc.™ Used by permission of Zondervan. All rights reserved worldwide. www.zondervan.com The "NIV" and "New International Version" are trademarks registered in the United States Patent and Trademark Office by Biblica, Inc.®

AMPC: Scripture taken from the Amplified Bible, Copyright © 1954, 1958, 1962, 1964, 1965, 1987 by The Lockman Foundation. Used by permission.

MEV: Scripture taken from the Modern English Version. Copyright © 2014 by Military Bible Association. Used by permission. All rights reserved.

Contents

BIG GOD
GETTING TO KNOW HIM

Introduction

Welcome!!! Here is a word of explanation. I began to envision a book to share with new believers. A book that pulls together verses of key points to assist after the new birth in Christ Jesus. The need for an outline or a skeleton of basic scriptures on which to build or refer to as they get their footing. I could not find exactly what I was looking for, so I have compiled these verses with thoughts and testimony to have available for you. Keep in mind this is a study tool to help you reach a place of understanding the foundations of Christianity (Matthew 7:24). Read with an inquiring mind and take your time, otherwise, you may be overwhelmed. Perseverance is key.

Remember that God will meet you where you are (Mark 2:16-17). Are you in the ditch? He is there. In the dark alley? He is there. Reach out to Him through genuine repentance and heartfelt prayer. He is only a whisper away. Are you on the mountaintop? He is there, too. Celebrate Him and whisper a prayer of thanksgiving.

It is very important to get connected with a church or fellowship of believers to attend their meetings (Acts 2:42). They are not all the same so caution is advised until you are sure of their core beliefs and values. Ask God to help you and He will. Internet meetings are a wonderful supplement and very readily available but once again use caution.

Who is God? He is BIG, UNFATHOMABLE and that is an impossible question to answer. There is not enough paper nor room on the earth to contain the books it would take to answer that question (John 21:25). Our human brains are not capable of processing the vastness of our Amazing Creator (Job 11:7). I will attempt to share basic Bible verses and thoughts to help you set foundational truths on which to build. These truths will help you along the way as you journey through life on the narrow road (Matthew 7:13-14).

One of the most important things I have learned along the way is to take any sermon, teaching, and even conversations about God and His word to personal study (1 Thessalonians 5:21; Matthew 7:15-16). Carefully guard your heart and mind against false understanding and error in interpretation (Proverbs 4:23; Philippians 4:6-7; Acts 17:11). It is a good principle to follow.

As you read your Bible try to do so without preconceived notions, but press in to fully understand each verse and passage as you go. What a verse speaks to you today may reveal other aspects and understandings the next time you read it (Proverbs 2:1-6). This may be because your relationship with the Holy Spirit is developing and you are learning to hear Him speak to you through various ways. Another reason is as we spiritually mature our understanding grows (Hebrews 4:12; Proverbs 30:5). We are also influenced by our journey which includes life events, experiences, challenges, and even traumas we may suffer. "Blessings to you and through you in Jesus' name!"

Donna L Bass

BIG GOD
GETTING TO KNOW HIM
Instructions

As you read and study your Bible, always note the action words in each verse. Try to grasp actions to embrace, and those to avoid. Make this a goal that you learn to implement in your daily walk. Also learn to use verses as prayers, incorporating them into your prayer list. Be sure to start a prayer list and if you tell someone you will pray for them, be careful to follow through.

The verses I have placed under each topic or heading are just a few of many. They are only the tip of the iceberg. Many of our topics and verses may overlap. If you find the repetition of some verses read from the perspective of the topic of the lesson or listed heading.

As you move along through the lessons you will develop more understanding. When you have something that speaks to your heart, stop there and dig awhile. The internet is an excellent tool for deeper study, but you must use caution in the selection of websites to avoid error. Take advantage of it! Searching by topic or cross-reference reading similar verses to increase your understanding. Remember this, if you cannot comprehend something use a good commentary or seek Godly counsel for clarity. Most importantly always remember Holy Spirit is with you and will teach you all things. Ask Him to help and He will.

Read each portion focused on the title subject, but don't overlook the other truths in the verses. I added a topic or heading to capture the theme of each lesson. Please observe in many of the comments and discussions there may be verses referenced throughout. These support the statements in which they are noted. As your time allows you, look them up, this will help you familiarize yourself with God's written Word, the Bible. Do not become overwhelmed, start small and grow from there. Read daily as you can, but don't go overboard or you may get overwhelmed and discouraged. No matter what, don't quit. Be persistent! Take baby steps and before you know it, you will be running.

It is crucial we do not take verses out of context which can bring misunderstanding and confusion (2 Peter 3:16; 2 Timothy 4:3-4). Always read the surrounding verses for clarity. I am old school and cherish a good study Bible and concordance. They are extremely useful and treasured assets. Consider reading verses aloud. This will involve not only your eyes but also your mouth and ears! Perhaps this will enhance recall and understanding. A whisper will be just fine.

DIVE IN

Lesson 1

God Is Big

Lesson Highlight:

> *For the LORD Most High is awesome, the great King*
> *over all the earth.*

— Psalm 47:2 NIV

Who is God? He is BIG and UNFATHOMABLE with innumerable facets we can spend a lifetime seeking to understand.

We must never consider ourselves to have a full understanding of Him (Ecclesiastes 8:16-17; 9:1). That is a place of pride and arrogance we must avoid (1 Corinthians 8:2). The more I learn, the more I realize I know nothing at all. I encourage you to press in! Pursue a relationship with your Amazing Creator (Psalm 42:1). He loves you and has a plan for your life (Jeremiah 29:11).

God is big! He not only occupies all time but space as well (Revelation 22:13; Jeremiah 23:24). He is vast, huge, and boundless (Job 38:1-41; Job 12:10). Like looking deep into the clear sky to which there is no end. Read small amounts at a time, allowing it to be absorbed into your heart. Also, keep in focus the lesson title and headings as you read.

HE IS GOD, KING AND LORD.

> But the LORD is the true God, he is the living God, and an ever-lasting king: at his wrath the earth shall tremble, and the nations shall not be able to abide his indignation.

> — Jeremiah 10:10 KJV

From the song Moses, the Israelites sang to the Lord:

> Who is like you, Yahweh, among the gods? Who is like you, glorious in holiness, Fearful in praises, doing wonders?

> — Exodus 15:11 WEB

Moses, as he was speaking to the people of Israel:

> For the Lord your God is God of gods and Lord of lords, the great God, mighty and awesome, who shows no partiality nor takes a bribe.

> — Deuteronomy 10:17 NKJV

> But our God is in the heavens: he hath done whatsoever he hath pleased.

> — Psalm 115:3 KJV

> For God is the King of all the earth. Sing praises with understanding. God reigns over the nations. God sits on his holy throne.

> — Psalm 47:7-8 WEB

AMAZING CREATOR

In the beginning God created the heaven and the earth.

— Genesis 1:1 KJV

Praise is the beginning of Jeremiah's prayer to the Lord:

Ah Lord GOD! behold, thou hast made the heaven and the earth by thy great power and stretched out arm, and there is nothing too hard for thee:

— Jeremiah 32:17 KJV

Thus says Yahweh, heaven is my throne, and the earth is my footstool: what manner of house will you build to me? and what place shall be my rest? For all these things has my hand made, and [so] all these things came to be, says Yahweh: but to this man will I look, even to him who is poor and of a contrite spirit, and who trembles at my word.

— Isaiah 66:1-2 WEB

A psalm of David:

By awesome deeds of righteousness, you answer us, God of our salvation. You who are the hope of all the ends of the earth, Of those who are far away on the sea; Who by his power forms the mountains, Having armed yourself with strength; Who stills the roaring of the seas, The roaring of their waves, And the turmoil of the nations.

— Psalm 65:5-7 WEB

In reference to Jesus Christ, Son of God:

> For by him were all things created, that are in heaven, and that are in earth, visible and invisible, whether they be thrones, or dominions, or principalities, or powers: all things were created by him, and for him:

— Colossians 1:16 KJV

HE IS EVERYWHERE

> Where can I go from your Spirit? Where can I flee from your presence? If I go up to the heavens, you are there; if I make my bed in the depths, you are there. If I rise on the wings of the dawn, if I settle on the far side of the sea, even there your hand will guide me, your right hand will hold me fast.

— Psalm 139:7-10 NIV

> But Jonah rose up to flee unto Tarshish from the presence of the LORD, and went down to Joppa; and he found a ship going to Tarshish: so he paid the fare thereof, and went down into it, to go with them unto Tarshish from the presence of the LORD. But the LORD sent out a great wind into the sea, and there was a mighty tempest in the sea, so that the ship was like to be broken.... So they took up Jonah, and cast him forth into the sea: and the sea ceased from her raging ... Now the LORD had prepared a great fish to swallow up Jonah. And Jonah was in the belly of the fish three days and three nights ... And the LORD spake unto the fish, and it vomited out Jonah upon the dry land.

— Jonah 1:3-4, 15, 17; 2:10 KJV

Am I a God at hand, saith the LORD, and not a God afar off? Can any hide himself in secret places that I shall not see him? saith the LORD. Do not I fill heaven and earth? saith the LORD.

— Jeremiah 23:23-24 KJV

MIGHTY IN POWER

All the earth will worship you, And will sing to you; They will sing to your name." Selah. Come, and see God's deeds -- Awesome work on behalf of the children of men. He turned the sea into dry land. They went through the river on foot. There, we rejoiced in him. He rules by his might forever. His eyes watch the nations. Don't let the rebellious rise up against him. Selah.

— Psalm 66:4-7 WEB

King Nebuchadnezzar's dream revealed by God to Daniel:

Then was the secret revealed unto Daniel in a night vision. Then Daniel blessed the God of heaven. Daniel answered and said, Blessed be the name of God for ever and ever: for wisdom and might are his: And he changeth the times and the seasons: he removeth kings, and setteth up kings: he giveth wisdom unto the wise, and knowledge to them that know understanding: He revealeth the deep and secret things: he knoweth what is in the darkness, and the light dwelleth with him.

— Daniel 2:19-22 KJV

And these are but the outer fringe of his works; how faint the whisper we hear of him! Who then can understand the thunder of his power?"

— Job 26:14 NIV

Great is our Lord, and of great power; his understanding is infinite.

— Psalm 147:5 KJV

While praying, Jehoshaphat said:

"LORD, the God of our ancestors, are you not the God who is in heaven? You rule over all the kingdoms of the nations. Power and might are in your hand, and no one can withstand you."

— 2 Chronicles 20:6 NIV

WISDOM AND KNOWLEDGE

Whom did the LORD consult to enlighten him, and who taught him the right way? Who was it that taught him knowledge or showed him the path of understanding? Surely the nations are like a drop in a bucket; they are regarded as dust on the scales; he weighs the islands as though they were fine dust ... Do you not know? Have you not heard? Has it not been told you from the beginning? Have you not understood since the earth was founded? He sits enthroned above the circle of the earth, and its people are like grasshoppers. He stretches out the heavens like a canopy, and spreads them out like a tent to live in.

— Isaiah 40:14-15, 21-22 NIV

Can anyone teach God knowledge, since He judges those who are on high?

— Job 21:22 MEV

that their hearts may be comforted, they being knit together in love, and to all riches of the full assurance of understanding, that they may know the mystery of God, both of the Father and of Christ, in whom are all the treasures of wisdom and knowledge hidden.

— Colossians 2:2-3 WEB

Oh, the depth of the riches both of the wisdom and knowledge of God! How unsearchable are His judgments and His ways past finding out! For who has known the mind of the Lord? Or who has become His counselor? Or who has first given to Him And it shall be repaid to him? For of Him and through Him and to Him are all things, to whom be glory forever. Amen.

— Romans 11:33-36 NKJV

Although God is vast and His ways unimaginable, He is concerned about every person. That includes you. Position yourself to grow in your relationship with Him through prayer and study. Start small and go from there. Diligence is necessary. Understanding that Christianity is a daily walk will be key to your growth. Two things to remember:

1. THE HEART: Your heart's condition and position regarding God.
2. TIME: It's not the quantity but the quality of the time you spend with Him.

HE IS PATIENT

The Lord is not slack concerning His promise, as some count slackness, but is longsuffering toward us, not willing that any should perish but that all should come to repentance.

— 2 Peter 3:9 NKJV

Do you despise the riches of His goodness, tolerance, and patience, not knowing that the goodness of God leads you to repentance?

— Romans 2:4 MEV

But I received mercy for this reason, that in me, first, Jesus Christ might show all patience, as an example to those who were to believe in Him for eternal life.

— 1 Timothy 1:16 MEV

PAUSE & PONDER

ARE YOU SETTLED AND CLEAR IN UNDERSTANDING THAT CREATIONISM IS THE TRUTH? THAT GOD CREATED ALL THINGS? The next verses will settle your mind and heart (Philippians 4:8).

Be still and know that I am God: I will be exalted among the heathen, I will be exalted in the earth.

— Psalm 46:10 KJV

Picture making a cup of hot tea. As you allow the tea bag to steep it changes the water into tea. The Bible, God's written Word, can act as a tea bag, as you read the Bible and think about the things of God, soaking awhile, opening your heart, little by little, you will become more like Him. One of my daily prayers that I pray for the lost is based on these next two verses.

For since the creation of the world His invisible attributes are clearly seen, being understood by the things that are made, even His eternal power and Godhead, so that they are without excuse,

— Romans 1:20 NKJV

The heavens declare the glory of God, and the firmament shows His handiwork. Day unto day utters speech, and night unto night declares knowledge. There is no speech and there are no words; their voice is not heard. Their line has gone out through all the earth, and their words to the end of the world. In them has He set a tent for the sun.

— Psalm 19:1-4 MEV

A PRAYER FOR YOU TO PRAY

"Father, I ask You to allow me to perceive the wonders and the workings of Your amazing creation. Let me see You in all that You have made, allowing faith to rise within me. Let Your goodness and love take root and spring forth from my heart. I ask this for the lost and backslidden too. Those who do not know You, Lord, open their eyes to see, ears to hear and hearts to understand who You are and that You love them, in Jesus' Name. Amen."

Lesson 2

He Is All That You Need

Lesson Highlight:

> *Don't you be afraid, for I am with you; don't be dismayed,*
> *for I am your God; I will strengthen you; yes, I will*
> *help you; yes, I will uphold you with the right hand*
> *of my righteousness ... For I, Yahweh your God, will*
> *hold your right hand, saying to you, Don't be afraid; I*
> *will help you.*
>
> — Isaiah 41:10, 13 WEB

As I worshiped this morning, the Lord took me back with a vision in my mind. Suddenly I was there in my childhood home underneath the covers on my bed. A little girl, me, crying out with tears flowing, pouring out my heart to my Amazing Creator. I could feel the warm tears on my face. I did not capture the words I spoke but the yearning of my heart as a child toward my heavenly Abba, Father God, was very clear (Isaiah 26:9a). You see, we have a relationship, Abba and I, we go way back. He longs for a relationship with you too (Proverbs 8:17).

Begin your journey today by turning to Him with your whole heart.

HE IS JUST, FAITHFUL AND HAS A PLAN

An excerpt from the Song of Moses:

> The Rock, his work is perfect; For all his ways are justice: A God of faithfulness and without iniquity, Just and right is he.

— Deuteronomy 32:4 WEB

Moses speaking to the people:

> Know therefore that the LORD thy God, he is God, the faithful God, which keepeth covenant and mercy with them that love him and keep his commandments to a thousand generations;

— Deuteronomy 7:9 KJV

> But if you will seek God earnestly and plead with the Almighty, if you are pure and upright, even now he will rouse himself on your behalf and restore you to your prosperous state. Your beginnings will seem humble, so prosperous will your future be.

— Job 8:5-7 NIV

> For I know the thoughts and plans that I have for you, says the Lord, thoughts and plans for welfare and peace and not for evil, to give you hope in your final outcome. Then you will call upon Me, and you will come and pray to Me, and I will hear and heed you. Then you will seek Me, inquire for, and require Me [as a vital necessity] and find Me when you search for Me with all your heart.

— Jeremiah 29:11-13 AMPC

Justice and judgment are the habitation of thy throne: mercy and truth shall go before thy face.

— Psalm 89:14 KJV

THE LORD YOUR GOD IS WITH YOU

The LORD is my shepherd, I shall not want.

— Psalm 23:1 KJV

The Lord said to Joshua:

Have I not commanded thee? Be strong and of good courage; be not afraid, neither be thou dismayed: for the LORD thy God is with thee whithersoever thou goest.

— Joshua 1:9 KJV

When the angel of the LORD appeared to Gideon, he said, "The LORD is with you, mighty warrior."

— Judges 6:12 NIV

HE IS YOUR SALVATION, STRONGHOLD AND CONFIDENCE

The LORD is my strength and song; and he is become my salvation: he is my God, and I will prepare him an habitation, my father's God, and I will exalt him.

— Exodus 15:2 KJV

The Lord is my light and my salvation; whom shall I fear? The Lord is the strength of my life; of whom shall I be afraid?

— Psalm 27:1 KJV

Yahweh is my rock, and my fortress, and my deliverer; My God, my rock, in whom I will take refuge; My shield, and the horn of my salvation, my high tower.

— Psalm 18:2 WEB

The LORD your God is with you, the Mighty Warrior who saves. He will take great delight in you; in his love he will no longer rebuke you, but will rejoice over you with singing.

— Zephaniah 3:17 NIV

I will lift up my eyes to the hills. Where does my help come from? My help comes from Yahweh, Who made heaven and earth. He will not allow your foot to be moved. He who keeps you will not slumber.

— Psalm 121:1-3 WEB

For You are my hope, O Lord God; You are my confidence from my youth.

— Psalm 71:5 MEV

HE IS LOVE, FULL OF GRACE AND COMPASSION

Whoever does not love does not know God, because God is love.

— 1 John 4:8 NIV

The LORD is gracious and full of compassion; slow to anger and of great mercy. The LORD is good to all: and his tender mercies are over all his works.

— Psalm 145:8-9 KJV

Yahweh is good, a stronghold in the day of trouble; and he knows those who take refuge in him.

— Nahum 1:7 WEB

Let us therefore come boldly unto the throne of grace, that we may obtain mercy, and find grace to help in time of need.

— Hebrews 4:16 KJV

And God is able to make all grace (every favor and earthly blessing) come to you in abundance, so that you may always and under all circumstances and whatever the need be self-sufficient [possessing enough to require no aid or support and furnished in abundance for every good work and charitable donation].

— 2 Corinthians 9:8 AMPC

HE CAN DO ALL THINGS

The Lord said to Abraham:

Is anything too difficult for the Lord? At the appointed time I will return to you, at this time next year, and Sarah will have a son."

— Genesis 18:14 MEV

Then Job answered Yahweh, "I know that you can do all things, And that no purpose of yours can be restrained.

— Job 42:1-2 WEB

Elisha speaking to the kings of Israel, Judah and Edom:

> For thus says the Lord: 'You shall not see wind, nor shall you see rain; yet that valley shall be filled with water, so that you, your cattle, and your animals may drink.' And this is a simple matter in the sight of the Lord; He will also deliver the Moabites into your hand.

— 2 Kings 3:17-18 NKJV

> And we know that all things work together for good to them that love God, to them who are the called according to his purpose.

— Romans 8:28 KJV

The angel, Gabriel, speaking to Mary:

> For with God nothing shall be impossible.

— Luke 1:37 KJV

> Jesus replied, "What is impossible with man is possible with God."

— Luke 18:27 NIV

THE GOD OF THE POSSIBLE

In 1996 I worked for a home health agency in a very small rural town and had completed a weekend of on-call visits. It was necessary to have all my paperwork in the office very early Monday morning since it had to be turned in for payroll completion. It was Sunday night after church and I was on the way to the office with my children when I started having car trouble.

I did have an old bag phone but no coverage in that area. The saying: "Don't go to the phone but run to the throne," was exactly what I needed to do (Psalm 17:6-7). And that's what we did. I prayed and asked for help from the Lord with my children in agreement (Psalm 50:15). We arrived at the office without difficulty. We locked ourselves in safely with a phone, bathroom, and snacks readily available.

My sister was able to pick us up and deliver us home. The culprit was a gaping hole in the water hose. As I have recalled that many times through the years, in my mind's eye I can see an angel flying alongside my car, his finger plugging the hole. I am grateful for provision and protection.

OUR AMAZING CREATOR IS ALL THAT YOU NEED!!!

God is our refuge and strength, a very present help in trouble.

— Psalm 46:1 KJV

Don't you be afraid, for I am with you; don't be dismayed, for I am your God; I will strengthen you; yes, I will help you; yes, I will uphold you with the right hand of my righteousness.

— Isaiah 41:10 WEB

Seeing that his divine power has granted to us all things that pertain to life and godliness, through the knowledge of him who called us by his own glory and virtue;

— 2 Peter 1:3 WEB

PAUSE & PONDER

DO YOU PRAY IN TIMES OF TROUBLE? HOW ABOUT WHEN YOU ARE BEING SQUEEZED BY LIFE'S CIRCUM-STANCES?

Run to Him through prayer. He is your refuge, strength, and help when you are in trouble. Run to Him!

> Is any among you suffering? Let him pray. Is any cheerful? Let him sing praises.
>
> — James 5:13 WEB

> But my God shall supply all your need according to his riches in glory by Christ Jesus.
>
> — Philippians 4:19 KJV

A PRAYER FOR YOU TO PRAY

"Father I thank You, that You are only a whisper away. Help me to always think of running to You first no matter the situation. Thank You for being my refuge, my strength, and my help when I am in trouble. I thank You for meeting all my needs according to Your glorious riches in Christ Jesus. Amen."

Lesson 3

He Is Unfathomable

Lesson Highlight:

> *Great is the LORD and most worthy of praise; his great-ness no one can fathom.*

> — Psalm 145:3 NIV

Another way to say this is: He cannot be measured, nor understood. Do not allow yourself to stumble if you cannot wrap your head around who God is. Just receive it by faith, believing what the Bible says (Genesis 15:6). Lingering with verses, chapters, or even books of the Bible will facilitate your understanding and bless you. (Psalm 1:1-3).

Focus on verses that grab your attention or speak to your heart. Take note of these and consider marking them in your Bible. There have been times I will read the same passages over and over until I gain understanding and get them deep in my heart (Joshua 1:8).

As you dig around in the Word and find those nuggets, write them down. If you study a particular topic, make notes. You will be glad as the years go by to have these on which to reflect.

HE CANNOT BE FATHOMED

Job, while speaking about God:

> Who does great things that can't be fathomed, Marvelous things without number;
>
> — Job 5:9 WEB

A psalmist, speaking about God:

> Such knowledge is too wonderful for me; It is high, I cannot attain it.
>
> — Psalm 139:6 NKJV

> "Can you fathom the mysteries of God? Can you probe the limits of the Almighty? They are higher than the heavens above—what can you do? They are deeper than the depths below—what can you know? Their measure is longer than the earth and wider than the sea."
>
> — Job 11:7-9 NIV

> Behold, God is great, and we know Him not! The number of His years is unsearchable.
>
> — Job 36:26 AMPC

HIS KNOWLEDGE AND WISDOM PROFOUND; HIS POWER VAST

To [the] only wise God be glory forevermore through Jesus Christ (the Anointed One)! Amen (so be it).

— Romans 16:27 AMPC

If one would dispute with Him, he cannot answer Him once in a thousand times. He is wise in heart and mighty in strength. Who has hardened himself against Him and prospered? He who does great things, beyond discovery, yes, and wonders beyond number.

— Job 9:3-4, 10 MEV

This also comes from the Lord of hosts, Who is wonderful in counsel [and] excellent in wisdom and effectual working.

— Isaiah 28:29 AMPC

Behold, God is exalted in his power. Who is a teacher like him? Who has prescribed his way for him? Or who can say, 'You have committed unrighteousness?'

— Job 36:22-23 WEB

Who hath directed the Spirit of the LORD, or being his counsellor hath taught him? With whom took he counsel, and who instructed him, and taught him in the path of judgment, and taught him knowledge, and shewed to him the way of understanding? To whom then will ye liken me, or shall I be equal? saith the Holy One ... Hast thou not known? hast thou not heard, that the everlasting God, the LORD, the Creator of the ends of the earth, fainteth not, neither is weary? there is no searching of his understanding.

—Isaiah 40:13-14, 25, 28 KJV

He counts the number of the stars. He calls them all by their names. Great is our Lord, and mighty in power. His understanding is infinite.

—Psalm 147:4-5 WEB

GREAT AND WONDERFUL IS HE AND HIS WORKS

Hear, oh, hear the roar of His voice and the sound of rumbling that goes out of His mouth! Under the whole heaven He lets it loose, and His lightning to the ends of the earth. After it His voice roars; He thunders with the voice of His majesty, and He restrains not [His lightnings against His adversaries] when His voice is heard. God thunders marvelously with His voice; He does great things which we cannot comprehend.

—Job 37:2-5 AMPC

How great are your works, LORD; how profound your thoughts!

—Psalm 92:5 NIV

I will meditate on the glorious splendor of Your majesty, And on Your wondrous works. Men shall speak of the might of Your awesome acts, And I will declare Your greatness

—Psalm 145:5-6 NKJV

Bless the LORD, O my soul. O LORD my God, thou art very great; thou art clothed with honour and majesty. Who coverest thyself with light as with a garment: who stretchest out the heavens like a curtain: Who layeth the beams of his chambers in the waters: who maketh the

clouds his chariot: who walketh upon the wings of the wind: Who
maketh his angels spirits; his ministers a flaming fire:

— Psalm 104:1-4 KJV

... which in its own times he will show, who is the blessed and only
Ruler, the King of kings, and Lord of lords; who alone has immortal-
ity, dwelling in unapproachable light; whom no man has seen, nor
can see: to whom be honor and eternal power. Amen.

— 1 Timothy 6:15-16 WEB

THE ON HIGH AND EXALTED ONE

For you, Yahweh, are most high above all the earth. You are exalted
far above all gods.

— Psalm 97:9 WEB

For thus says the high and lofty One who inhabits eternity, whose
name is Holy: I dwell in the high and holy place, with him also who is
of a contrite and humble spirit, to revive the spirit of the humble, and
to revive the heart of the contrite.

— Isaiah 57:15 WEB

For my thoughts are not your thoughts, neither are your ways my
ways, saith the LORD. For as the heavens are higher than the earth, so
are my ways higher than your ways, and my thoughts than your
thoughts.

— Isaiah 55:8-9 KJV

Speaking of Jesus:

> Behold, my servant shall deal wisely, he shall be exalted and lifted up, and shall be very high.
>
> — Isaiah 52:13 WEB

EVERYTHING

> There is a time for everything, and a season for every activity under the heavens ... He has made everything beautiful in its time. He has also set eternity in the human heart; yet no one can fathom what God has done from beginning to end.
>
> — Ecclesiastes 3:1,11 NIV

The Lord said to Job:

> Who has first given to me, that I should repay him? Everything under the heavens is mine.
>
> — Job 41:11 WEB

> I heard every created thing which is in heaven, on the earth, under the earth, on the sea, and everything in them, saying, "To him who sits on the throne, and to the Lamb be the blessing, the honor, the glory, and the dominion, forever and ever. Amen." The four living creatures said, "Amen!" The elders fell down and worshiped.
>
> — Revelation 5:13-14 WEB

HIS WONDERS

Remember his marvelous works that he hath done; his wonders, and the judgments of his mouth;

— Psalm 105:5 KJV

O LORD my God, You have done many wonderful works, and Your thoughts toward us cannot be compared; if I would declare and speak of them, they are more than can be numbered.

— Psalm 40:5 MEV

"You men of Israel, hear these words. Jesus of Nazareth, a man approved by God to you by mighty works and wonders and signs which God did by him in the midst of you, even as you yourselves know ..."

— Acts 2:22 WEB

TESTIFY

In my early twenties, I went with my church youth group as a chaperone on a retreat. The Lord moved hearts and there were many commitments by participants. As we sat out in the clear open, under the star-speckled sky the Lord seemed to confirm His joy and pleasure with a fantastic show of shooting stars. The first one or two caught our attention but as they continued we sat in awe of what seemed to be His confirmation of the decisions made. He had His eye on a small group from South Mississippi and sent us a light show in the stars to reveal to us He was pleased.

HE IS TRULY UNFATHOMABLE!!!
(Psalm 19:1; Psalm 89:5; Psalm 148)

PAUSE & PONDER

ARE YOU WATCHING CAREFULLY FOR THE WORKINGS OF GOD IN YOUR LIFE?

Try to expand your perception of things and keep your mind positioned to recognize Him at work in your life. He knows you, everything about you. From Him nothing can be hidden, not your thoughts and certainly not your deeds.

> Neither is there any creature that is not manifest in his sight: but all things are naked and opened unto the eyes of him with whom we have to do.
>
> — Hebrews 4:13 KJV

> For nothing is secret, that shall not be made manifest; neither any thing hid, that shall not be known and come abroad.
>
> — Luke 8:17 KJV

You may see Him at work in your family, circumstances, or job. He may speak to you through His Word, a billboard, or even a light show of shooting stars. Always listen. Incline your ears to hear what He is saying.

> So shall my word be that goes forth out of my mouth: it shall not return to me void, but it shall accomplish that which I please, and it shall prosper in the thing whereto I sent it.
>
> — Isaiah 55:11 WEB

For God does speak—now one way, now another—though no one perceives it.

— Job 33:14 NIV

A PRAYER FOR YOU TO PRAY

"Father, I thank You for speaking to me one way and another. Help me to be perceptive and to recognize You in whatever way You are speaking or moving in my life, in Jesus Name, Amen."

Lesson 4

The Trinity ... Three Yet One

Lesson Highlights:
Romans 1:20-21 KJV
Colossians 2:1-3 KJV
Acts 17:29-31 KJV

THE GODHEAD

For the invisible things of him from the creation of the world are clearly seen, being understood by the things that are made, even his eternal power and Godhead; so that they are without excuse: Because that, when they knew God, they glorified him not as God, neither were thankful; but became vain in their imaginations, and their foolish heart was darkened.

— Romans 1:20-21 KJV

For I would that ye knew what great conflict I have for you, and for them at Laodicea, and for as many as have not seen my face in the flesh; That their hearts might be comforted, being knit together in love, and unto all riches of the full assurance of understanding, to the acknowledgement of the mystery of God, and of the Father, and of Christ; In whom are hid all the treasures of wisdom and knowledge.

— Colossians 2:1-3 KJV

Forasmuch then as we are the offspring of God, we ought not to think that the Godhead is like unto gold, or silver, or stone, graven by art and man's device. And the times of this ignorance God winked at; but now commandeth all men every where to repent: Because he hath appointed a day, in the which he will judge the world in right-eousness by that man whom he hath ordained; whereof he hath given assurance unto all men, in that he hath raised him from the dead.

— Acts 17:29-31 KJV

MADE IN GOD'S IMAGE ...

Refers to God, His Spirit and uses plural "our image:"

In the beginning God created the heavens and the earth. Now the earth was formless and empty. Darkness was on the surface of the deep. God's Spirit was hovering over the surface of the waters ... God said, "Let us make man in our image, after our likeness: and let them have dominion over the fish of the sea, and over the birds of the sky, and over the cattle, and over all the earth, and over every creeping thing that creeps on the earth."

— Genesis 1:1-2, 26 WEB

But we all, with open face beholding as in a glass the glory of the Lord, are changed into the same image from glory to glory, even as by the Spirit of the Lord.

— 2 Corinthians 3:18 KJV

Receive the Trinity by faith. It is a hard concept to grasp and understand, but remember this:

" ... big
... big
...BIG
GOD
... little tiny human brain "

Through the years I have seen a few people who allowed their inability to grasp and understand this concept stumble. It seemed as though they could not move forward in their faith. Faith is believing (Romans 10:17; Hebrews 11:1). Believing God is...and He is, who He says He is.

YOU MUST BELIEVE!!!
(James 2:19; John 20:29; Mark 9:23)

The next text is the first and fourth verses from an old hymn that was written by Reginald Heber in 1826 titled "Holy, Holy, Holy! Lord God

Almighty!" Notice the last line in each verse, it may explain it in a way that may be easier to understand:

GOD IN THREE PERSONS, BLESSED TRINITY!

Holy, holy, holy! Lord God almighty!
Early in the morning our song shall rise to thee.
Holy, holy, holy! Merciful and mighty!
God in three persons, blessed trinity!

Holy, holy, holy! Lord God almighty!
All thy works shall praise thy name,
in earth, and sky, and sea.
Holy, holy, holy! Merciful and mighty!
God in three persons, blessed trinity!

THE LORD IS GOD

To you it was shown, that you might know that Yahweh he is God; there is none else besides him ... Know therefore this day, and lay it to your heart, that Yahweh he is God in heaven above and on the earth beneath; there is none else.

— Deuteronomy 4:35, 39 WEB

This was a small thing in your eyes, God; but you have spoken of your servant's house for a great while to come, and have regarded me according to the estate of a man of high degree, Yahweh God ... Yahweh, there is none like you, neither is there any God besides you, according to all that we have heard with our ears.

— 1 Chronicles 17:17, 20 WEB

"You are my witnesses," declares the LORD, "and my servant whom I have chosen, so that you may know and believe me and understand that I am he. Before me no god was formed, nor will there be one after me. I, even I, am the LORD, and apart from me there is no savior. I have revealed and saved and proclaimed— I, and not some foreign god among you. You are my witnesses," declares the LORD, "that I am God. Yes, and from ancient days I am he. No one can deliver out of my hand. When I act, who can reverse it?"

— Isaiah 43:10-13 NIV

THE LORD IS ONE

Hear, O Israel: The LORD our God is one LORD:

— Deuteronomy 6:4 KJV

Therefore concerning the eating of things sacrificed to idols, we know that no idol is anything in the world, and that there is no other God but one. For though there are things that are called "gods," whether in the heavens or on earth; as there are many "gods" and many "lords;" yet to us there is one God, the Father, of whom are all things, and we to him; and one Lord, Jesus Christ, through whom are all things, and we through him.

— 1 Corinthians 8:4-6 WEB

You believe that there is one God. You do well. Even the demons believe--and tremble!

— James 2:19 NKJV

There is one body, and one Spirit, even as ye are called in one hope of your calling; One Lord, one faith, one baptism, One God and Father of all, who is above all, and through all, and in you all.

— Ephesians 4:4-6 KJV

DAISY CHAIN

Read the next three verses as if they are daisy-chained together.

God said to Moses:

He said, "You cannot see My face, for no man can see Me and live.

— Exodus 33:20 MEV

Jesus answered the Jews:

I and my Father are one.

— John 10:30 KJV

Speaking of Jesus:

For in Him dwells all the fullness of the Godhead bodily;

— Colossians 2:9 NKJV

As revealed in the prior three verses, our God is so very big that Jesus came to make the fullness of GOD known to us. Receive it by faith and remember:

"... BIG
... BIG
...BIG GOD"

THE SON OF GOD...GOD WITH US

The angel, Gabriel, speaking to Mary:

> Then the angel said to her, The Holy Spirit will come upon you, and the power of the Most High will overshadow you [like a shining cloud]; and so the holy (pure, sinless) Thing (Offspring) which shall be born of you will be called the Son of God.

> — Luke 1:35 AMPC

Now all this was done, that it might be fulfilled which was spoken of the Lord by the prophet, saying, Behold, a virgin shall be with child, and shall bring forth a son, and they shall call his name Emmanuel, which being interpreted is, God with us.

— Matthew 1:22-23 KJV

In the beginning was the Word, and the Word was with God, and the Word was God. He was with God in the beginning ... The Word became flesh and made his dwelling among us. We have seen his glory, the glory of the one and only Son, who came from the Father, full of grace and truth ... No one has ever seen God, but the one and only Son, who is himself God and is in closest relationship with the Father, has made him known.

— John 1:1-2, 14, 18 NIV

HOLY SPIRIT DESCENDED AND IS DEPOSITED

Now when all the people were baptized, it came to pass, that Jesus also being baptized, and praying, the heaven was opened, And the Holy Ghost descended in a bodily shape like a dove upon him, and a voice came from heaven, which said, Thou art my beloved Son; in thee I am well pleased.

— Luke 3:21-22 KJV

Now He who establishes us with you in Christ and has anointed us is God, who also has sealed us and given us the Spirit in our hearts as a guarantee.

— 2 Corinthians 1:21-22 NKJV

GOD THE FATHER, GOD THE SON, AND GOD THE HOLY SPIRIT

Verses where Father, Son, and Holy Spirit are mentioned together.

> Philip said to him, "Lord, show us the Father, and that will be enough for us."
>
> Jesus said to him, "Have I been with you such a long time, and do you not know me, Philip? He who has seen me has seen the Father. How do you say, 'Show us the Father?' Don't you believe that I am in the Father, and the Father in me? The words that I tell you, I speak not from myself; but the Father living in me does his works.
>
> Believe me that I am in the Father, and the Father in me; or else believe me for the very works' sake ... If you love me, keep my commandments. I will pray to the Father, and he will give you another Counselor, that he may be with you forever,— the Spirit of truth, whom the world can't receive; for it doesn't see him, neither knows him. You know him, for he lives with you, and will be in you. I will not leave you orphans. I will come to you.

— John 14:8-11; 15-18 WEB

Jesus speaking to His disciples:

> But the Comforter (Counselor, Helper, Intercessor, Advocate, Strengthener, Standby), the Holy Spirit, Whom the Father will send in My name [in My place, to represent Me and act on My behalf], He will teach you all things. And He will cause you to recall (will remind you of, bring to your remembrance) everything I have told you.

— John 14:26 AMPC

Jesus speaking:

> But if I cast out devils by the Spirit of God, then the kingdom of God
> is come unto you.
>
> — Matthew 12:28 KJV

> But when the Comforter (Counselor, Helper, Advocate, Intercessor,
> Strengthener, Standby) comes, Whom I will send to you from the
> Father, the Spirit of Truth Who comes (proceeds) from the Father,
> He [Himself] will testify regarding Me.
>
> — John 15:26 AMPC

Jesus speaking to His disciples after the resurrection:

> And being assembled together with them, He commanded them not
> to depart from Jerusalem, but to wait for the Promise of the Father,
> "which," He said, "you have heard from Me; for John truly baptized
> with water, but you shall be baptized with the Holy Spirit not many
> days from now."
>
> — Acts 1:4-5 NKJV

> The grace of the Lord Jesus Christ, and the love of God, and the
> communion of the Holy Spirit be with you all. Amen.
>
> — 2 Corinthians 13:14 MEV

> But now in Christ Jesus you who were formerly far away have been
> brought near through the blood of Christ ... For by Him we both have
> access by one Spirit to the Father. Now, therefore, you are no longer

strangers and foreigners, but are fellow citizens with the saints and members of the household of God ...

— Ephesians 2:13, 18-19 MEV

TRINITY...TRI MEANS THREE...FATHER, SON, and HOLY SPIRIT.

TRINITY: THREE INDIVIDUALS, YET ONE;

ONE REALLY BIG, BIG, BIG GOD!!

GOD IN THREE PERSONS BLESSED TRINITY!

Without controversy, the mystery of godliness is great: God was revealed in the flesh, Justified in the spirit, Seen by angels, Preached among the nations, Believed on in the world, And received up in glory.

— 1 Timothy 3:16 WEB

Whoever denies the Son, the same doesn't have the Father. He who confesses the Son has the Father also.

— 1 John 2:23 WEB

PAUSE & PONDER

CAN YOU COMPREHEND THIS?

Remember do not allow this to cause you to stumble. Just receive it by faith and go forward (Luke 3:22; John 1:32; Matthew 3:17; Matthew 17:5).

Trinity...three yet one...Father, Son, and Holy Spirit...the Godhead.

Jesus speaking:

> Go ye therefore, and teach all nations, baptizing them in the name of the Father, and of the Son, and of the Holy Ghost
>
> — Matthew 28:19 KJV

A PRAYER FOR YOU TO PRAY

"Father, I ask that You help me to believe and settle it in my heart that You are a big God, so big that You are three yet one. Help me receive it by faith in Jesus' name. Amen."

Lesson 5

God The Father

Lesson Highlight:

> *Yet for us there is but one God, the Father, from whom all things came and for whom we live; and there is but one Lord, Jesus Christ, through whom all things came and through whom we live.*

> — 1 Corinthians 8:6 NIV

I was so blessed to have had a wonderful earthly father that loved God and loved his family. Unfortunately, through the years I have come to realize many people have not had the love of an earthly father. Abusive, neglectful, and self-centered parents are more the norm, especially today.

If this is the case for you, it will take effort to understand that you have an amazing Father, God the Father, and He loves you. Our heavenly Father is a good, good Father who cares for you. He is always there for you. Anywhere, everywhere and all the time! Reach out to Him by seeking Him through worship, prayer, and Bible study.

OUR FATHER

For you are our Father, though Abraham doesn't know us, and Israel does not acknowledge us: you, Yahweh, are our Father; our Redeemer from everlasting is your name.

— Isaiah 63:16 WEB

But now, Yahweh, you are our Father; we are the clay, and you our potter; and we all are the work of your hand.

— Isaiah 64:8 WEB

And the LORD God formed man of the dust of the ground, and breathed into his nostrils the breath of life; and man became a living soul.

— Genesis 2:7 KJV

This is the book of the generations of Adam. In the day that God created man, he made him in God's likeness. He created them male and female, and blessed them, and called their name Adam, in the day when they were created.

— Genesis 5:1-2 WEB

Scripture calls Adam, "son of God." It also calls Jesus the "Son of God." Jesus, the One and Only-begotten Son is the fullness of God. (John 1:1, 14, 18; John 3:16, Colossians 2:9)

Which was the son of Enos, which was the son of Seth, which was the son of Adam, which was the son of God.

— Luke 3:38 KJV

Every good and perfect gift is from above, coming down from the Father of the heavenly lights, who does not change like shifting shadows. He chose to give us birth through the word of truth, that we might be a kind of firstfruits of all he created.

— James 1:17-18 NIV

Blessed be the God and Father of our Lord Jesus Christ, who hath blessed us with all spiritual blessings in heavenly places in Christ

— Ephesians 1:3 KJV

FATHER OF ALL AND IN ALL

Don't we all have one father? Hasn't one God created us?

— Malachi 2:10a WEB

One God and Father of all, who is above all, and through all, and in you all.

— Ephesians 4:6 KJV

FATHER AND HIS CHILDREN

Beloved, let us love one another, for love is of God; and everyone who loves is born of God, and knows God. He who doesn't love doesn't know God, for God is love.

— 1 John 4:7-8 WEB

For as many as are led by the Spirit of God, they are the sons of God. For ye have not received the spirit of bondage again to fear; but ye have received the Spirit of adoption, whereby we cry, "Abba Father."

— Romans 8:14-15 KJV

What agreement has a temple of God with idols? For you are a temple of the living God. Even as God said, "I will dwell in them, and walk in them; and I will be their God, and they will be my people."

Therefore, "'Come out from among them, And be separate,' says the Lord, 'Touch no unclean thing. I will receive you. I will be to you a Father. You will be to me sons and daughters,' says the Lord Almighty."

— 2 Corinthians 6:16-18 WEB

The LORD is compassionate and gracious, slow to anger, abounding in love ... As a father has compassion on his children, so the LORD has compassion on those who fear him; for he knows how we are formed, he remembers that we are dust."

— Psalm 103:8, 13-14 NIV

My son, do not despise the LORD's discipline, and do not resent his rebuke, because the LORD disciplines those he loves, as a father the son he delights in.

— Proverbs 3:11-12 NIV

FATHER SENT JESUS AND HOLY SPIRIT

Jesus speaking to Nicodemus:

"For God so loved the world, that he gave his only begotten Son, that whosoever believeth in him should not perish, but have everlasting life."

— John 3:16 KJV

But God demonstrates His own love toward us, in that while we were still sinners, Christ died for us.

— Romans 5:8 NKJV

Jesus teaching the disciples:

If you then, being evil, know how to give good gifts to your children, how much more will your heavenly Father give the Holy Spirit to those who ask Him?"

— Luke 11:13 MEV

And we are witnesses of these things, and the Holy Spirit is also, Whom God has bestowed on those who obey Him.

— Acts 5:32 AMPC

JESUS SPEAKS TO AND OF THE FATHER

Jesus teaching Sermon on the Mount:

But you, when you pray, enter into your inner chamber, and having shut your door, pray to your Father who is in secret, and your Father who sees in secret will reward you openly ... Therefore don't be like them, for your Father knows what things you need, before you ask him. Pray like this.

'Our Father, who is in heaven, may your name be kept holy. May your kingdom come. May your will be done, as in heaven, so on earth. Give us this day our daily bread. Forgive us our debts, as we also forgive our debtors. Bring us not into temptation, but deliver us from evil. For yours is the kingdom, the power and the glory forever. Amen.'

— Matthew 6:6, 8-13 WEB

Jesus in Gethsemane:

He went forward a little, and fell on the ground, and prayed that, if it were possible, the hour might pass away from him. He said, "Abba, Father, all things are possible to you. Please remove this cup from me. However, not what I want, but what you want."

— Mark 14:35-36 WEB

Jesus speaking:

In my Father's house are many mansions: if it were not so, I would have told you. I go to prepare a place for you."

— John 14:2 KJV

Jesus speaking:

Fear not, little flock; for it is your Father's good pleasure to give you the kingdom.

— Luke 12:32 KJV

FATHER AND DEFENDER

O Lord, You have heard the desire and the longing of the humble and oppressed; You will prepare and strengthen and direct their hearts, You will cause Your ear to hear, to do justice to the fatherless and the oppressed, so that man, who is of the earth, may not terrify them any more.

— Psalm 10:17-18 AMPC

The Lord protects and preserves the strangers and temporary residents, He upholds the fatherless and the widow and sets them upright, but the way of the wicked He makes crooked (turns upside down and brings to ruin.

— Psalm 146:9 AMPC

A father of the fatherless, and a protector of the widows, is God in His holy habitation.

— Psalm 68:5 MEV

In the above verse, Psalm 68:5 MEV declares God is "A father to the fatherless, a protector of widows." He has a special place for them in His heart as also stated in the next verse. Be mindful of this and give them help whenever possible.

Religion that is pure and undefiled before God, the Father, is this: to visit the fatherless and widows in their affliction and to keep oneself unstained by the world.

— James 1:27 MEV

I remember my parents visiting several of the elderly widows in our church putting up handrails where needed around their homes to assist them in avoiding falls. Even the smallest of things are greatly appreciated when you need help. Sometimes knowing someone cares enough to help and is willing to demonstrate God's love can mend a wounded heart.

Always without fail point to God. Any glory gleaned through your life must always point to God, giving Him His glory.

My parents also supported the Baptist Children's Village through the years and my sister married a man who had been raised in one from a nearby state. I keenly remember Daddy voicing he felt they had gleaned a son from the seed they had sown. They gained a son and my brother-in-law gained a family. We loved him dearly.

Our God is a good Father! Seek Him (Matthew 7:7). Embrace Him and allow Him into your life. He will never leave you nor forsake you (Deuteronomy 31:8; Hebrews 4:16). Pursue a relationship with Him every day (1 Chronicles 16:11). Pray, confess your sins, and repent (Colossians 4:2). Keep your slate clean with daily repentance (1 John 1:9; Acts 3:19).

PAUSE & PONDER

DO YOU HAVE THE ABILITY TO UNDERSTAND AND RECEIVE THE LOVE OF THE FATHER?

One of the most precious parables Jesus told was the story of the prodigal son (Luke 15:11-32). It conveys the wild rebellious actions of a son as well as the forgiveness and love of his father. It is a picture of God's sons and daughters when we backslide and our amazing heavenly Father who is always there for us when we turn our hearts to Him. Run quickly to your heavenly Father. He will meet you where you are, even coming out of a pigpen.

Jesus telling the parable:

And he arose and came to his father. But when he was still a great way off, his father saw him and had compassion, and ran and fell on his neck and kissed him.

— Luke 15:20 NKJV

Yahweh appeared of old to me, [saying], Yes, I have loved you with an everlasting love: therefore with lovingkindness have I drawn you.

— Jeremiah 31:3 WEB

A PRAYER YOU CAN PRAY

"Father help me to perceive the love You have for me. Help me understand it cannot be earned, but You freely give it to all who will receive. Thank You for Your love, Father. Amen."

Lesson 6

The Ways Of God

Lesson Highlight:
   Moses said to the Lord:

> *Now therefore, if I have found favor in your sight, please*
> *show me now your ways, that I may know you, so*
> *that I may find favor in your sight: and consider that*
> *this nation is your people.*

> — Exodus 33:13 WEB

Think of studying a map for direction, way, or a course in which to travel. Now shift your vision and perception to not only these verses but all of God's Scriptures. Follow His ways as you live your life according to His Word.

As you read and study, examine your life, and pay attention to the action words. Be mindful and embrace those you are instructed to do, but diligently avoid those you are directed not to do.

UNSEARCHABLE

O the depth of the riches both of the wisdom and knowledge of God! how unsearchable are his judgments, and his ways past finding out!

— Romans 11:33 KJV

For my thoughts are not your thoughts, neither are your ways my ways, saith the Lord. For as the heavens are higher than the earth, so are my ways higher than your ways, and my thoughts than your thoughts.

— Isaiah 55:8-9 KJV

As I have pondered and studied the ways of God, there are too many to include in a short lesson. His ways are His manner, method, and characteristics. Different resources have a variety of interpretations. Remember to take any teaching or interpretation to the Lord in prayer.

"Way" defined by Merriam-Webster.com:

1. The course traveled from one place to another
2. A course leading in a direction or toward an objective
3. Manner or method of doing or happening
4. Characteristic, regular, or habitual manner or mode of being, behaving or happening

Then the LORD said, "Shall I hide from Abraham what I am about to do? Abraham will surely become a great and powerful nation, and all the nations on earth will be blessed through him. For I have chosen him, so that he will direct his children and his household after him to keep the way of the LORD by doing what is right and just, so that the LORD will bring about for Abraham what he has promised him."

— Genesis 18:17-19 NIV

He leads the humble in what is right, and the humble He teaches His way.

— Psalm 25:9 AMPC

But he knows the way that I take. When he has tried me, I shall come forth like gold. My foot has held fast to his steps. His way have I kept, and not turned aside. I haven't gone back from the commandment of his lips. I have treasured up the words of his mouth more than my necessary food.

— Job 23:10-12 WEB

SHOW US YOUR WAYS

A Psalm of David:

Show me your ways, Yahweh. Teach me your paths. Guide me in your truth, and teach me, For you are the God of my salvation, I wait for you all day long ... Good and upright is Yahweh, Therefore he will instruct sinners in the way. He will guide the humble in justice. He will teach the humble his way. All the paths of Yahweh are lovingkindness and truth To such as keep his covenant and his testimonies.

— Psalm 25:4-5, 8-10 WEB

Teach me your way, O Lord, that I will walk in Your truth; bind my heart to fear your name.

— Psalm 86:11 MEV

HIS WAYS

His ways are the path we must take as we walk out our lives yielding to the instructions set forth in the Bible. Read with the goal to glean the ways of God as you move through the lesson. This is only the tip of the iceberg. Remember, we have learned He is unfathomable.

Now therefore, I pray, if I have found grace in Your sight, show me now Your way, that I may know You and that I may find grace in Your sight. And consider that this nation is Your people." And he said, "Please, show me Your glory." Then He said, "I will make all My goodness pass before you, and I will proclaim the name of the Lord before you. I will be gracious to whom I will be gracious, and I will have compassion on whom I will have compassion."

— Exodus 33:13, 18-19 NKJV

The Lord executes righteousness And justice for all who are oppressed. He made known His ways to Moses, His acts to the children of Israel. The Lord is merciful and gracious, Slow to anger, and abounding in mercy... But the mercy of the Lord is from everlasting to everlasting On those who fear Him, And His righteousness to children's children, To such as keep His covenant, And to those who remember His commandments to do them.

— Psalm 103:6-8, 17-18 NKJV

Wash yourselves, make yourselves clean; put away the evil of your doings from before My eyes! Cease to do evil, Learn to do right! Seek justice, relieve the oppressed, and correct the oppressor. Defend the fatherless, plead for the widow.

— Isaiah 1:16-17 AMPC

From the Song of Moses:

For I will proclaim the name of Yahweh: Ascribe greatness to our God. The Rock, his work is perfect; For all his ways are justice: A God of faithfulness and without iniquity, Just and right is he.

— Deuteronomy 32:3-4 WEB

KEEP HIS COMMANDMENTS

Now, Israel, what does Yahweh your God require of you, but to fear Yahweh your God, to walk in all his ways, and to love him, and to serve Yahweh your God with all your heart and with all your soul, to keep the commandments of Yahweh, and his statutes, which I command you this day for your good?

— Deuteronomy 10:12-13 WEB

If/then verse, God says if you do this, then I will do that:

The Lord will establish you as a holy people to Himself, just as He has sworn to you, if you keep the commandments of the Lord your God and walk in His ways.

— Deuteronomy 28:9 NKJV

But take diligent heed to do the commandment and the law, which Moses the servant of the LORD charged you, to love the LORD your God, and to walk in all his ways, and to keep his commandments, and to cleave unto him, and to serve him with all your heart and with all your soul.

— Joshua 22:5 KJV

... but I gave them this command: Obey me, and I will be your God and you will be my people. Walk in obedience to all I command you, that it may go well with you. But they did not listen or pay attention; instead, they followed the stubborn inclinations of their evil hearts. They went backward and not forward.

— Jeremiah 7:23-24 NIV

If you keep my commandments, you will remain in my love; even as I have kept my Father's commandments, and remain in his love.

— John 15:10 WEB

... teaching them to observe all things which I commanded you. Behold, I am with you always, even to the end of the age." Amen.

— Matthew 28:20 WEB

YOU WILL FIND REST, PEACE, AND REFUGE

This is what the LORD says: "Stand at the crossroads and look; ask for the ancient paths, ask where the good way is, and walk in it, and you will find rest for your souls. But you said, 'We will not walk in it.'

— Jeremiah 6:16 NIV

This is what the LORD says—your Redeemer, the Holy One of Israel: "I am the LORD your God, who teaches you what is best for you, who directs you in the way you should go. If only you had paid attention to my commands, your peace would have been like a river, your well-being like the waves of the sea."

— Isaiah 48:17-18 NIV

As for God, his way is perfect: The LORD's word is flawless; he shields all who take refuge in him.

— Psalm 18:30 NIV

THE SECRET PLACE

Through the years I have sent brief Bible studies to friends and family members. There were two topics I kept going back to: "entering the rest of God" and "the peace of God." Residing in the rest, peace and quietness of who God is in your life is a place. It is the secret place.

He who dwells in the shelter of the Most High shall abide under the shadow of the Almighty.

— Psalm 91:1 MEV

The fear of Yahweh leads to life, then contentment; He rests and will not be touched by trouble.

— Proverbs 19:23 WEB

But godliness with contentment is great gain. For we brought nothing into this world, and it is certain we can carry nothing out.

— 1 Timothy 6:6-7 KJV

For unto us a child is born, unto us a son is given: and the government shall be upon his shoulder: and his name shall be called Wonderful, Counsellor, The mighty God, The everlasting Father, The Prince of Peace.

— Isaiah 9:6 KJV

Not that I am implying that I was in any personal want, for I have learned how to be content (satisfied to the point where I am not disturbed or disquieted) in whatever state I am. I know how to be abased and live humbly in straitened circumstances, and I know also how to enjoy plenty and live in abundance. I have learned in any and all circumstances the secret of facing every situation, whether well-fed or going hungry, having a sufficiency and enough to spare or going without and being in want. I have strength for all things in Christ Who empowers me [I am ready for anything and equal to anything through Him Who infuses inner strength into me; I am self-sufficient in Christ's sufficiency].

— Philippians 4:11-13 AMPC

Jesus speaking:

"Come to Me, all you who labor and are heavily burdened, and I will give you rest. Take My yoke upon you, and learn from Me. For I am meek and lowly in heart, and you will find rest for your souls. For My yoke is easy, and My burden is light."

— Matthew 11:28-30 MEV

Rejoice in the Lord always. Again I will say, rejoice! Let everyone come to know your gentleness. The Lord is at hand. Be anxious for nothing, but in everything, by prayer and supplication with gratitude, make your requests known to God. And the peace of God, which surpasses all understanding, will protect your hearts and minds through Christ Jesus.

— Philippians 4:4-7 MEV

These are places of spiritual maturity. It is the place of casting your cares on Him no matter the circumstance (1 Peter 5:7; Psalm 55:22). A quiet place that you know you are in the palm of His hand and that He cares for you (Philippians 4:6; Isaiah 49:16; Deuteronomy 31:8).

I AM RUNNING FOR THE SECRET PLACE!!!!
LEARNING TO REST IN HIM NO MATTER WHAT THE
CIRCUMSTANCES!!!
THANK YOU JESUS!!!

PAUSE AND PONDER

ARE YOU LISTENING FOR HIM? LEARNING TO RECOGNIZE THOSE WHISPERS AND SUBTLE PROMPTINGS? (Job 33:14-16; 1 Kings 19:11-13)

Although the Lord gives you the bread of adversity and the water of affliction, your teachers will be hidden no more; with your own eyes you will see them. Whether you turn to the right or to the left, your ears will hear a voice behind you, saying, "This is the way; walk in it."

— Isaiah 30:20-21 NIV

Call to me, and I will answer you, and will show you great things, and difficult, which you don't know.

— Jeremiah 33:3 WEB

Jesus speaking:

But he answered them, "My mother and my brothers are these who hear the word of God, and do it."

— Luke 8:21 WEB

So faith comes by hearing, and hearing by the word of God.

— Romans 10:17 WEB

My sheep hear my voice, and I know them, and they follow me.

— John 10:27 WEB

A PRAYER YOU CAN PRAY

"Father, I ask for wisdom and also for discernment. Help me to understand and to walk in Your ways. Reveal to me any rebellion or stubbornness that I may have in my life or heart, in Jesus' name."

> *Who is wise? Let them realize these things. Who is discerning? Let them understand. The ways of the LORD are right; the righteous walk in them, but the rebellious stumble in them.*

— Hosea 14:9 NIV

Lesson 7
The Will, Purpose, And Plan Of God

Lesson Highlights:
Matthew 18:12-14 AMPC
Luke 19:10 KJV

Jesus speaking to His disciples:

> What do you think? If a man has a hundred sheep, and one of them has gone astray and gets lost, will he not leave the ninety-nine on the mountain and go in search of the one that is lost? And if it should be that he finds it, truly I say to you, he rejoices more over it than over the ninety-nine that did not get lost. Just so it is not the will of My Father Who is in heaven that one of these little ones should be lost and perish.
>
> — Matthew 18:12-14 AMPC

Jesus speaking to Zacchaeus:

For the Son of man is come to seek and save that which was lost.

— Luke 19:10 KJV

HIM WHO SEES

It is our Father's will that each person repents and receives Jesus as their Lord and Savior. He has a purpose and plan for everyone. One of my favorite stories in the Bible is the story of Hagar, the servant of Sarai. God was up close and personal with this broken servant girl. Sarai thought she had a great idea to have children for Abram by her servant, Hagar. Once Hagar was pregnant the sparks flew and after being mistreated, Hagar ran away. The angel of the Lord found her near a spring in the desert. Let's look at a few of these verses:

> Now the Angel of the Lord found her by a spring of water in the wilderness, by the spring on the way to Shur. And He said, "Hagar, Sarai's maid, where have you come from, and where are you going?" She said, "I am fleeing from the presence of my mistress Sarai..." And the Angel of the Lord said to her: "Behold, you are with child, And you shall bear a son. You shall call his name Ishmael, Because the Lord has heard your affliction ... Then she called the name of the Lord who spoke to her, You-Are-the-God-Who-Sees; for she said, "Have I also here seen Him who sees me?"

— Genesis 16:7-8, 11,13 NKJV

After Isaac was born to Abraham and Sarah conflict arose, Hagar and her son were sent away.

> God heard the voice of the boy. The angel of God called to Hagar out of the sky, and said to her, "What ails you, Hagar? Don't be afraid. For God has heard the voice of the boy where he is. Get up, lift up the

boy, and hold him in your hand. For I will make him a great nation." God opened her eyes, and she saw a well of water. She went, filled the bottle with water, and gave the boy drink.

— Genesis 21:17-19 WEB

These encounters bless my heart and are some of my favorite passages. "The God who sees." How amazing, He cares for the least of these. He sees and cares for all and that includes you. Our Amazing Creator loves you so. Reach out to Him. Pursue a relationship with Him. You will never regret it for He is the God who sees you.

GOD'S WILL

Jesus speaking at the Sermon on the Mount:

After this manner therefore pray ye: Our Father which art in heaven, Hallowed be thy name. Thy kingdom come. Thy will be done in earth, as it is in heaven.

— Matthew 6:9-10 KJV

Look carefully then how you walk! Live purposefully and worthily and accurately, not as the unwise and witless, but as wise (sensible, intelligent people) Making the very most of the time [buying up each opportunity], because the days are evil. Therefore do not be vague and thoughtless and foolish, but understanding and firmly grasping what the will of the Lord is.

— Ephesians 5:15-17 AMPC

He who searches the hearts knows what is on the Spirit's mind, because he makes intercession for the saints according to God.

— Romans 8:27 WEB

KNOWING AND DOING HIS WILL

Teach me to do your will, For you are my God. Your Spirit is good. Lead me in the land of uprightness.

— Psalm 143:10 WEB

And do not be conformed to this world, but be transformed by the renewing of your mind, that you may prove what is that good and acceptable and perfect will of God.

— Romans 12:2 NKJV

HIS WILL FOR US

Rejoice always. Pray without ceasing. In everything give thanks, for this is the will of God in Christ Jesus toward you.

— 1 Thessalonians 5:16-18 WEB

It is God's will that you should be sanctified: that you should avoid sexual immorality; that each of you should learn to control your own body in a way that is holy and honorable, not in passionate lust like the pagans, who do not know God; and that in this matter no one should wrong or take advantage of his brother or sister. The Lord will punish all those who commit such sins, as we told you and warned you before. For God did not call us to be impure, but to live a holy life. Therefore, anyone who rejects this instruction does not reject a human being but God, the very God who gives you his Holy Spirit.

— 1 Thessalonians 4:3-8 NIV

For so is the will of God, that by well-doing you should put to silence the ignorance of foolish men

— 1 Peter 2:15 WEB

Don't love the world, neither the things that are in the world. If anyone loves the world, the Father's love isn't in him. For all that is in the world, the lust of the flesh, the lust of the eyes, and the pride of life, isn't the Father's, but is the world's. The world is passing away with its lusts, but he who does God's will remains forever.

— 1 John 2:15-17 WEB

CHRIST DID THE FATHER'S WILL

David's Psalm also speaks of Jesus:

Then I said, "Behold, I have come. It is written about me in the book in the scroll. I delight to do your will, my God. Yes, your law is within my heart."

— Psalm 40:7-8 WEB

Grace to you and peace from God the Father, and our Lord Jesus Christ, who gave himself for our sins, that he might deliver us out of this present evil age, according to the will of our God and Father --to whom be the glory forever and ever. Amen.

— Galatians 1:3-5 WEB

PERSEVERE EVEN THROUGH SUFFERING

For you need patience, so that, having done the will of God, you may receive the promise.

— Hebrews 10:36 WEB

And let us not lose heart and grow weary and faint in acting nobly and doing right, for in due time and at the appointed season we shall reap, if we do not loosen and relax our courage and faint.

— Galatians 6:9 AMPC

So then, let those who suffer according to the will of God entrust their souls to a faithful Creator, while continuing to do good.

— 1 Peter 4:19 MEV

THE LORD'S PURPOSE

For when God made [His] promise to Abraham, He swore by Himself, since He had no one greater by whom to swear ...Accordingly God also, in His desire to show more convincingly and beyond doubt to those who were to inherit the promise the unchangeableness of His purpose and plan, intervened (mediated) with an oath.

— Hebrews 6:13, 17 AMPC

The Lord says:

So shall my word be that goeth forth out of my mouth: it shall not return unto me void, but it shall accomplish that which I please, and it shall prosper in the thing whereto I sent it.

— Isaiah 55:11 KJV

Remember the former things, those of long ago; I am God, and there is no other; I am God, and there is none like me. I make known the end from the beginning, from ancient times, what is still to come. I say, 'My purpose will stand, and I will do all that I please.'

— Isaiah 46:9-10 NIV

The counsel of the Lᴏʀᴅ stands forever, the purposes of His heart to all generations.

— Psalm 33:11 MEV

And we know that all things work together for good to them that love God, to them who are the called according to his purpose.

— Romans 8:28 KJV

So do not be ashamed of the testimony of our Lord, nor of me, His prisoner. But share in the sufferings of the gospel by the power of God, who has saved us and called us with a holy calling, not by our works, but by His own purpose and grace, which was given us in Christ Jesus before the world began.

— 2 Timothy 1:8-9 MEV

GOD HAS A PLAN

I know that you can do all things, And that no purpose of yours can be restrained.

— Job 42:2 WEB

He has a plan!

Trust in the Lord with all thine heart; and lean not unto thine own understanding. In all thy ways acknowledge him, and he shall direct thy paths.

— Proverbs 3:5-6 KJV

Don't you be afraid, for I am with you; don't be dismayed, for I am your God; I will strengthen you; yes, I will help you; yes, I will uphold you with the right hand of my righteousness.

— Isaiah 41:10 WEB

The LORD Almighty has sworn, "Surely, as I have planned, so it will be, and as I have purposed, so it will happen.

— Isaiah 14:24 NIV

AND A BACKUP PLAN

The next verse gives us great revelation and insight into God's goodness and His faithfulness. This is one you need to ponder, teach intently to your children, and put in your back pocket. It makes us aware that when we are tempted He will provide a way out of the situation, helping us to avoid giving in to temptation.

No temptation has taken you except what is common to man. God is faithful, and He will not permit you to be tempted above what you can endure, but will with the temptation also make a way to escape, that you may be able to bear it.

— 1 Corinthians 10:13 MEV

Let's look at this same verse in the Amplified Bible also.

For no temptation (no trial regarded as enticing to sin), [no matter how it comes or where it leads] has overtaken you and laid hold on you that is not common to man [that is, no temptation or trial has come to you that is beyond human resistance and that is not adjusted and adapted and belonging to human experience, and such as man can bear]. But God is faithful [to His Word and to His compassionate nature], and He [can be trusted] not to let you be tempted and tried and assayed beyond your ability and strength of resistance and power to endure, but with the temptation He will [always] also provide the way out (the means of escape to a landing place), that you may be capable and strong and powerful to bear up under it patiently.

— 1 Corinthians 10:13 AMPC

When I was a teenager, I got into a situation where the door opened for me to avoid sinning against the Lord. Unaware of this verse, I did not perceive the door - nor walk through this access to escape temptation. Much later I repented, and knew the Lord forgave me.

I am grateful to have learned about this amazing provision from God., and am determined when temptation arises to immediately look for the escape the Lord will provide. I have decided ahead of time to dash for the door. We should teach this to whomever we have the opportunity to. Perhaps if they perceive the door it may awaken them to see the need to flee from temptation.

"Thank You, Lord, for the door of escape, the landing place and help me run through it whenever I am tempted In Jesus' name. Amen."

Then the Lord knows how to rescue the godly from trial, and to keep the unrighteous under punishment for the Day of Judgment.

— 2 Peter 2:9 MEV

JESUS IS THE PURPOSE AND THE PLAN

Jesus speaking:

> For God so loved the world, that he gave his only begotten Son, that whosoever believeth in him should not perish, but have everlasting life.
>
> — John 3:16 KJV

Peter preaching on the Day of Pentecost:

> "Men of Israel, hear these words: Jesus of Nazareth, a Man attested by God to you by miracles, wonders, and signs which God did through Him in your midst, as you yourselves also know-- Him, being delivered by the determined purpose and foreknowledge of God, you have taken by lawless hands, have crucified, and put to death;"
>
> — Acts 2:22-23 NKJV

> This is good, and pleases God our Savior, who wants all people to be saved and to come to a knowledge of the truth.
>
> — 1 Timothy 2:3-4 NIV

> The Lord is not slow concerning His promise, as some count slowness. But He is patient with us, because He does not want any to perish, but all to come to repentance.
>
> — 2 Peter 3:9 MEV

> For I know the thoughts that I think toward you, says the Lord, thoughts of peace and not of evil, to give you a future and a hope.

Then you will call upon Me and go and pray to Me, and I will listen to you. And you will seek Me and find Me, when you search for Me with all your heart.

— Jeremiah 29:11-13 NKJV

CONSIDER THIS

God brought the children of Israel out of Egypt with the plan of bringing them to the land He promised Abraham. A land flowing with milk and honey. After spying out the land they were unwilling to go in because of the giants and large walled cities there. They did not trust God, became arrogant, and rebelled. They also murmured and the Lord heard them (Deuteronomy 1:19-46). Their sin resulted in death after wandering forty years in the desert (Joshua 5:6-7).

God does not just see you where you are at any given time but also where you have been and where you are going. He knows the beginning from the end (Psalm 139:13-16; Jeremiah 1:4-5; Isaiah 41:4).

He loves you (John 3:16; Romans 5:8). He has a plan, a purpose, and a perfect will for your life (Isaiah 41:10; Jeremiah 29:11; Psalm 57:2; Romans 12:2). Seek Him and submit to His will. His will is good for you (Matthew 11:28-30; 1 John 2:17; 1 Thessalonians 4:3-8).

PAUSE AND PONDER

CAN YOU WRAP YOUR BRAIN AROUND THE KNOWLEDGE THAT YOUR AMAZING CREATOR LOVES AND CARES FOR YOU? HE ALSO LOVES, DELIGHTS IN, AND SINGS OVER YOU?

The LORD your God is in your midst, a Mighty One, who will save. He will rejoice over you with gladness, He will renew you with His love, He will rejoice over you with singing.

— Zephaniah 3:17 MEV

A PRAYER YOU CAN PRAY

One of my prayer verses:

"Father, help me to place my trust and confidence in You, O Lord. I ask that Your will, purpose, and plan for my life will be fulfilled, in Jesus' Name. Amen."

Blessed is the man who trusts in the Lord, And whose hope is the Lord.

— Jeremiah 17:7 NKJV

Lesson 8

God The Son, Jesus Christ

Lesson Highlight:

> *But Jesus kept silent. And the high priest said to Him, I call upon you to swear by the living God, and tell us whether you are the Christ, the Son of God. Jesus said to him, You have stated [the fact]. More than that, I tell you: You will in the future see the Son of Man seated at the right hand of the Almighty and coming on the clouds of the sky.*
>
> — Matthew 26:63-64 AMPC

BELIEVE AND GET TO KNOW HIM

"Believe" defined by Merriam-Webster.com

1. Transitive verb: to consider to be true or honest
2. Intransitive verb: to have a firm or wholehearted religious conviction
3. Persuasion; to regard the existence of God as a fact

The Bible explains that without faith it is impossible to please God and that those who wish to draw near to Him must believe He exists (Hebrews 11:6). It also reveals that the cross is foolishness to the lost (1 Corinthians 1:18). It is easy to see the importance of planting the seeds of the Gospel along the way (Matthew 13:3-9; 1 Corinthians 3:6-9). We must train our children and grandchildren in the ways of God and His wonderful plan of redemption through Jesus (Deuteronomy 12:19; Psalm 78:4).

"Faith" defined by Merriam-Webster.com:

1. Noun: belief in and loyalty to God
2. Noun: firm belief in something especially with strong conviction
3. Verb: believe, trust

Jesus said to him, "Because you have seen me, you have believed. Blessed are those who have not seen, and have believed." Therefore Jesus did many other signs in the presence of his disciples, which are not written in this book; but these are written, that you may believe that Jesus is the Christ, the Son of God, and that believing you may have life in his name.

— John 20:29-31 WEB

The Son of God, Jesus Christ, came to His created earth as a newborn baby (Isaiah 7:14). He suffered many things, and we too will suffer (1 Peter 4:12-19). He was tempted as we are tempted, yet He was without sin (Hebrews 4:15).

THE GATE

Jesus speaking at the Sermon on the Mount:

Enter in by the narrow gate; for wide is the gate, and broad is the way, that leads to destruction, and many are those who enter in by it. How narrow is the gate, and restricted is the way that leads to life! Few are those who find it.

— Matthew 7:13-14 WEB

Jesus said:

I am the gate; whoever enters through me will be saved. They will come in and go out and find pasture.

— John 10:9 NIV

Father God has provided a way to enter into a relationship with Him. The Way is JESUS (John 14:6). Salvation is available to everyone but not everyone will be saved. It's a choice and YOU MUST CHOOSE!!! (Mark 8:34; Joshua 24:15; John 1:12-13)

BEFORE ABRAHAM WAS BORN, I AM!

Jesus said to them, "Most assuredly, I tell you, before Abraham was born, I AM."

— John 8:58 WEB

In Exodus 3:13 Moses asked God what he should tell the Israelites when they ask the name of the God of their fathers who sent him. His answer is in the next verse.

God said to Moses, "I AM WHO I AM," and he said, "You shall tell the children of Israel this: "I AM has sent me to you."

— Exodus 3:14 WEB

As we look at the book of John we see Jesus used the term I AM in referring to Himself. Look and see these very powerful statements.

I am the bread of life (John 6:35).

I am the light of the world (John 8:12).

I am the gate (John 10:7, 9).

I am the good shepherd (John 10:11, 14).

I am the resurrection and the life (John 11:25).

I am the way, the truth, and the life (John 14:6).

I am the true vine (John 15:1, 5).

THE WORD...THE ONE AND ONLY!!!

The book of John, one of my favorite books, refers to Jesus as the Word and describes Him as the one and only. It brings joy and excitement to my heart every time I read these verses.

> In the beginning was the Word, and the Word was with God, and the Word was God. He was with God in the beginning ... The Word became flesh and made his dwelling among us. We have seen his glory, the glory of the one and only Son, who came from the Father, full of grace and truth ... No one has ever seen God, but the one and only Son, who is himself God and is in closest relationship with the Father, has made him known.
>
> — John 1:1-2, 14,18 NIV

THE ONE AND ONLY....LOOK AGAIN AND GET HAPPY!!!

Jesus speaking to Nicodemus:

> As Moses lifted up the serpent in the wilderness, even so must the Son of Man be lifted up, that whoever believes in him should not perish, but have eternal life. For God so loved the world, that he gave his one and only Son, that whoever believes in him should not perish,

but have eternal life. For God didn't send his Son into the world to judge the world, but that the world should be saved through him. He who believes in him is not judged. He who doesn't believe has been judged already, because he has not believed in the name of the only born Son of God.

— John 3:14-18 WEB

A CHILD IS BORN...A SON IS GIVEN.

Now, let's take a look back at the Old Testament. The next passages are from Isaiah's prophecy of Jesus and were written around 700 years before His birth.

For unto us a child is born, unto us a son is given: and the government shall be upon his shoulder: and his name shall be called Wonderful, Counsellor, The mighty God, The everlasting Father, The Prince of Peace. Of the increase of his government and peace there shall be no end, upon the throne of David, and upon his kingdom, to order it, and to establish it with judgment and with justice from henceforth even for ever. The zeal of the LORD of hosts will perform this.

— Isaiah 9:6-7 KJV

And there shall come forth a shoot from the stump of Jesse, and a Branch shall grow out of his roots. The Spirit of the LORD shall rest upon him, the Spirit of wisdom and understanding, the Spirit of counsel and might, the Spirit of knowledge and of the fear of the LORD. He shall delight in the fear of the LORD, and he shall not judge by what his eyes see, nor reprove by what his ears hear; but with righteousness he shall judge the poor, and reprove with fairness for the meek of the earth. He shall strike the earth with the rod of his mouth, and with the breath of his lips he shall slay the wicked. Righteousness shall be the belt of his loins, and faithfulness the belt about his waist.

— Isaiah 11:1-5 MEV

HE IS THE IMAGE OF THE INVISIBLE GOD, THE RADIANCE OF GOD'S GLORY.

No man hath seen God at any time; the only begotten Son, which is in the bosom of the Father, he hath declared him.

— John 1:18 KJV

He is the image of the invisible God, the firstborn over all creation.

— Colossians 1:15 NKJV

God, who at various times and in various ways spoke in time past to the fathers by the prophets, has in these last days spoken to us by His Son, whom He has appointed heir of all things, through whom also He made the worlds; who being the brightness of His glory and the express image of His person, and upholding all things by the word of His power, when He had by Himself purged our sins, sat down at the right hand of the Majesty on high,

— Hebrews 1:1-3 NKJV

DO NOT DOUBT BUT BELIEVE

"Doubt" defined by Merriam-Webster.com:

1. Noun: an inclination not to believe or accept
2. Transitive verb: to call into question the truth of
3. Intransitive verb: to be uncertain

If you had known Me, you would have known My Father also. From now on you do know Him and have seen Him." Philip said to Him,

"Lord, show us the Father, and that is sufficient for us." Jesus said to him, "Have I been with you such a long time, and yet you have not known Me, Philip? He who has seen Me has seen the Father. So how can you say, 'Show us the Father'? Do you not believe that I am in the Father and the Father is in Me? The words that I say to you I do not speak on My own authority. But the Father who lives in Me does the works. Believe Me that I am in the Father, and the Father is in Me. Or else believe Me on account of the works themselves.

— John 14:7-11 MEV

But Thomas, one of the twelve, called Didymus, wasn't with them when Jesus came. The other disciples therefore said to him, "We have seen the Lord!" But he said to them, "Unless I see in his hands the print of the nails, and put my hand into his side, I will not believe." After eight days again his disciples were within, and Thomas with them. Jesus came, the doors being locked, and stood in the midst, and said, "Peace be to you." Then he said to Thomas, "Reach here your finger, and see my hands. Reach here your hand, and put it into my side. Don't be faithless, but believing." Thomas answered him, "My Lord and my God!"

— John 20:24-28 WEB

We know that the Son of God has come, and has given us an understanding, that we know him who is true, and we are in him who is true, in his Son Jesus Christ. This is the true God, and eternal life.

— 1 John 5:20 WEB

PETER KNEW HIM, THE SON OF GOD!!!

Now when Jesus came into the parts of Caesarea Philippi, he asked his disciples, saying, "Who do men say that I, the Son of Man, am?"

They said, "Some say John the Baptizer, some, Elijah, and others, Jeremiah, or one of the prophets." He said to them, "But who do you say that I am?" Simon Peter answered, "You are the Christ, the Son of the living God." Jesus answered him, "Blessed are you, Simon Bar-jonah, for flesh and blood has not revealed this to you, but my Father who is in heaven.

— Mathew 16:13-17 WEB

And Peter answered Him, Lord, if it is You, command me to come to You on the water. He said, Come! So Peter got out of the boat and walked on the water, and he came toward Jesus. But when he perceived and felt the strong wind, he was frightened, and as he began to sink, he cried out, Lord, save me [from death]! Instantly Jesus reached out His hand and caught and held him, saying to him, O you of little faith, why did you doubt? And when they got into the boat, the wind ceased. And those in the boat knelt and worshiped Him, saying, Truly You are the Son of God!

— Matthew 14:28-33 AMPC

HE HAS ALL AUTHORITY, OUR BLESSED HOPE.

Then Jesus came to them and said, "All authority in heaven and on earth has been given to me. Therefore go and make disciples of all nations, baptizing them in the name of the Father and of the Son and of the Holy Spirit, and teaching them to obey everything I have commanded you. And surely I am with you always, to the very end of the age."

— Matthew 28:18-20 NIV

Then comes the end, when He delivers the kingdom to God the Father, when He puts an end to all rule and all authority and power.

For He must reign till He has put all enemies under His feet. The last enemy that will be destroyed is death.

— 1 Corinthians 15:24-26 NKJV

Looking for the blessed hope and glorious appearing of our great God and Savior Jesus Christ, who gave Himself for us, that He might redeem us from every lawless deed and purify for Himself His own special people, zealous for good works.

— Titus 2:13-14 NKJV

GOD THE SON, JESUS CHRIST, CAME AS A MAN TO HIS CREATION TO REDEEM THAT WHICH WAS LOST THROUGH THE SIN OF ADAM AND EVE.
(Colossians 1:16; Luke 19:10; Romans 5:12)

HE CAME IN HUMILITY AND LOVE.
(Philippians 2:8; John 3:16)

CHOOSING TO SERVE OTHERS RATHER THAN BE SERVED.
(John 13:3-5; Mark 10:45)

HE CAME AS THE LAMB OF GOD TO DIE ON THE CROSS AND SAVE US FROM OUR SINS.
(John 1:29; John 19:17-18; Hebrews 9:22)

JESUS, JESUS, JESUS THERE IS POWER IN HIS NAME
(Philippians 2:9-11; Luke 10:17)

THERE IS LOVE, JOY, AND PEACE IN HIM
(John 15:11-23; John 14:27).

GET TO KNOW HIM BY SITTING AT HIS FEET
(John 12:3; Luke 10:39)

PAUSE & PONDER

CAN YOU BELIEVE AND RECEIVE THIS AS TRUTH?
PERHAPS YOU ARE ASKING: "HOW CAN THIS BE?"

Let's look closely at the question: "How can this be?" Mary, the Mother of Jesus, asked this of the angel who visited her. Also, Nicodemus, a Pharisee, asks this of Jesus. Read on.

MARY ASKED

And Mary said to the angel, How can this be, since I have no [intimacy with any man as a] husband? Then the angel said to her, The Holy Spirit will come upon you, and the power of the Most High will overshadow you [like a shining cloud]; and so the holy (pure, sinless) Thing (Offspring) which shall be born of you will be called the Son of God.

— Luke 1:34-35 AMPC

NICODEMUS ASKED

Jesus answered him, "Most assuredly, I tell you, unless one is born anew, he can't see the kingdom of God." Nicodemus said to him, "How can a man be born when he is old? Can he enter a second time into his mother's womb, and be born?" Jesus answered, "Most assuredly I tell you, unless one is born of water and the Spirit, he can't enter into the kingdom of God! That which is born of the flesh is flesh. That which is born of the Spirit is spirit. Don't marvel that I said to you, 'You must be born anew.' The wind blows where it wants to, and you hear its sound, but don't know where it comes from and where it is going. So is everyone who is born of the Spirit." Nicodemus answered him, "How can these things be?"

— John 3:3-9 WEB

A PRAYER YOU CAN PRAY

"Lord, open the eyes of my heart. Remove doubt and help me to believe. To believe You spoke, by Your word, everything into existence. That You formed Adam from the dust of the ground. And yes, the virgin birth of Jesus the Christ. Lord help my unbelief in Jesus' Name. Amen."

And the LORD God formed man of the dust of the ground, and breathed into his nostrils the breath of life; and man became a living soul.

— Genesis 2:7 KJV

Lesson 9

The Ministry Of Jesus

Lesson Highlight:

> *As they were eating, Jesus took bread, gave thanks for it,*
> *and broke it. He gave to the disciples, and said,*
> *"Take, eat; this is my body." He took the cup, gave*
> *thanks, and gave to them, saying, "Drink all of it, for*
> *this is my blood of the new covenant, which is*
> *poured out for many for the remission of sins. But I*
> *tell you that I will not drink of this fruit of the vine*
> *from now on, until that day when I drink it anew*
> *with you in my Father's kingdom."*

> — Matthew 26:26-29 WEB

O, taste and see that the Lord is good (Psalm 34:8 KJV; Psalm 119:103). Nothing else will satisfy (Psalm 107:9; John 6:35). So many of us waste our lives trying to find what will truly satisfy but we look in the wrong places (Galatians 5:19-21; 1 John 2:15-17). We at various times will turn to sinful pleasures that do not last (Job 20:5; Proverbs

14:12) and will destroy our lives mentally, physically, and emotionally (James 1:14-15; Romans 6:16). Say NO to sin.

JESUS IS THE ANSWER!!! JESUS IS THE ONLY WAY!!!

Jesus saith unto him, I am the way, the truth, and the life: no man cometh unto the Father, but by me.

— John 14:6 KJV

When our Amazing Creator made man, our purpose was to proclaim His praise (Isaiah 43:21; Psalm 63:5). He requires that we do justice, love kindness, and walk humbly with Him (Leviticus 26:12; Micah 6:8). We are His temple, with a place inside us that only He can fill (2 Corinthians 6:16; Revelation 21:3).

SAVIOR

"Savior" synonyms by Merriam-Webster.com

1. deliver
2. redeemer
3. rescuer

Jesus our Savior, Deliverer, and Rescuer is an ever-present help in times of trouble (Psalm 46:1). For those who receive Him, He will always be with you. His Spirit, the Holy Spirit, lives in you (Isaiah 41:10; 1 Corinthians 3:16). He will never leave you nor forsake you (Deuteronomy 31:6).

And we have seen and do testify that the Father sent the Son to be the Saviour of the world.

— 1 John 4:14 KJV

For unto you is born this day in the city of David a Saviour, which is Christ the Lord.

— Luke 2:11 KJV

Be it known to you all, and to all the people of Israel, that in the name of Jesus Christ of Nazareth, whom you crucified, whom God raised from the dead, in him does this man stand here before you whole. He is 'the stone which was regarded as worthless by you, the builders, which was made the head of the corner.' There is salvation in none other, for neither is there any other name under heaven, that is given among men, in which we must be saved!"

— Acts 4:10-12 WEB

For this is good and acceptable in the sight of God our Saviour; Who will have all men to be saved, and to come unto the knowledge of the truth.

— 1 Timothy 2:3-4 KJV

DELIVERER aka RESCUER

... and so all Israel will be saved. Even as it is written, "There will come out of Zion the Deliverer, And he will turn away ungodliness from Jacob. This is my covenant to them, When I will take away their sins."

— Romans 11:26-27 WEB

The Lord is my rock and my fortress and my deliverer; My God, my strength, in whom I will trust; My shield and the horn of my salvation, my stronghold.

— Psalm 18:2 NKJV

He rescued me from my powerful enemy, from my foes, who were too strong for me ... He brought me out into a spacious place; he rescued me because he delighted in me.

— Psalm 18:17, 19 NIV

"Listen to me, you descendants of Jacob, all the remnant of the people of Israel, you whom I have upheld since your birth, and have carried since you were born. Even to your old age and gray hairs I am he, I am he who will sustain you. I have made you and I will carry you; I will sustain you and I will rescue you."

— Isaiah 46:3-4 NIV

REDEEMER

Thus says Yahweh, the King of Israel, and his Redeemer, Yahweh of Hosts: I am the first, and I am the last; and besides me there is no God.

— Isaiah 44:6 WEB

For thy Maker is thine husband; the LORD of hosts is his name; and thy Redeemer the Holy One of Israel; The God of the whole earth shall he be called.

— Isaiah 54:5 KJV

THE FULLNESS

Giving thanks unto the Father, which hath made us meet to be partakers of the inheritance of the saints in light: Who hath delivered us from the power of darkness, and hath translated us into the kingdom of his dear Son: In whom we have redemption through his blood, even the forgiveness of sins: Who is the image of the invisible God, the firstborn of every creature: For by him were all things created, that are in heaven, and that are in earth, visible and invisible, whether they be thrones, or dominions, or principalities, or powers: all things were created by him, and for him: And he is before all things, and by him all things consist. And he is the head of the body, the church: who is the beginning, the firstborn from the dead; that in all things he might have the preeminence. For it pleased the Father that in him should all fulness dwell; And, having made peace through the blood of his cross, by him to reconcile all things unto himself; by him, I say, whether they be things in earth, or things in heaven.

— Colossians 1:12-20 KJV

But to each one of us grace was given according to the measure of Christ's gift. And He Himself gave some to be apostles, some prophets, some evangelists, and some pastors and teachers, for the equipping of the saints for the work of ministry, for the edifying of the body of Christ, till we all come to the unity of the faith and of the knowledge of the Son of God, to a perfect man, to the measure of the stature of the fullness of Christ.

— Ephesians 4:7, 11-13 NKJV

PROPHET'S WORDS FULFILLED

He came to Nazareth, where he had been brought up. He entered, as was his custom, into the synagogue on the Sabbath day, and stood up to read. The book of the prophet Isaiah was handed to him. He opened the book, and found the place where it was written, "The Spirit of the Lord is on me, Because he anointed me to preach good news to the poor. He has sent me to heal the brokenhearted, To proclaim release to the captives, Recovering of sight to the blind, To deliver those who are crushed, And to proclaim the acceptable year of the Lord. He closed the book, gave it back to the attendant, and sat down. The eyes of all in the synagogue were fastened on him. He began to tell them, "Today, this Scripture has been fulfilled in your hearing."

— Luke 4:16-21 WEB

But God raised Him on the third day and presented Him publicly, not to all the people, but to witnesses previously chosen by God, to us who ate and drank with Him after He rose from the dead. He commanded us to preach to the people and to testify that it is He who was ordained by God to be the Judge of the living and the dead. To Him all the prophets bear witness that whoever believes in Him will receive remission of sins through His name."

— Acts 10:40-43 MEV

THOUGH RICH, HE BECAME A SERVANT

I have pondered the following verses many times. The precious, One and Only Son of God left the magnificence of heaven and willingly came to this earth, His creation, to die. He was mistreated, scorned, mocked, beaten, crucified, and died for us. He came to redeem those who choose to receive the wonderful gift of His salvation. Receive Him today.

Who, being in the form of God, did not consider equality with God something to be grasped. But He emptied Himself, taking upon Himself the form of a servant, and was made in the likeness of men. And being found in the form of a man, He humbled Himself and became obedient to death, even death on a cross. Therefore God highly exalted Him and gave Him the name which is above every name, that at the name of Jesus every knee should bow, of those in heaven and on earth and under the earth, and every tongue should confess that Jesus Christ is Lord, to the glory of God the Father.

— Philippians 2:6-11 MEV

Jesus speaking to His disciples:

"It shall not be so among you, but whoever would become great among you will be your servant. Whoever would be first among you will be your bondservant, even as the Son of Man came not to be served, but to serve, and to give his life as a ransom for many."

— Matthew 20:26-28 WEB

[That] Jesus, knowing (fully aware) that the Father had put everything into His hands, and that He had come from God and was [now] returning to God, got up from supper, took off His garments, and taking a [servant's] towel, He fastened it around His waist. Then He poured water into the washbasin and began to wash the disciples' feet and to wipe them with the [servant's] towel with which He was girded.

— John 13:3-5 AMPC

For you know the grace of our Lord Jesus Christ, that, though he was rich, yet for your sakes he became poor, that you through his poverty might become rich.

— 2 Corinthians 8:9 WEB

HE HEALED THEM

After one of my granddaughters was born she repeatedly failed the hearing tests. My daughter and son-in-law were at that time lukewarm at best but both knew exactly what to do. They ran to the Lord's feet crying out for their daughter's ears to be healed and He did just that. The Lord's touch made her hearing ability completely whole.

The Lord desires to heal. Reach out like the woman pressing quietly through the crowd touching his garment, and instantly she received her healing (Matthew 9:18-26).

> Jesus went about in all Galilee, teaching in their synagogues, preaching the gospel of the kingdom, and healing every disease and every sickness among the people. The report about him went forth into all Syria. They brought to him all who were sick, afflicted with various diseases and torments, possessed with demons, epileptics, and paralytics; and he healed them.
>
> — Matthew 4:23-24 WEB

> When evening came, they brought to Him many who were under the power of demons, and He drove out the spirits with a word and restored to health all who were sick. And thus He fulfilled what was spoken by the prophet Isaiah, He Himself took [in order to carry away] our weaknesses and infirmities and bore away our diseases.
>
> — Matthew 8:16-17 AMPC

> And Jesus summoned to Him His twelve disciples and gave them power and authority over unclean spirits, to drive them out, and to cure all kinds of disease and all kinds of weakness and infirmity. Jesus sent out these twelve, charging them, Go nowhere among the Gentiles and do not go into any town of the Samaritans; But go rather to the lost sheep of the house of Israel. And as you go, preach, saying, The kingdom of heaven is at hand! Cure the sick, raise the dead,

cleanse the lepers, drive out demons. Freely (without pay) you have received, freely (without charge) give.

— Matthew 10:1, 5-8 AMPC

When they had crossed over, they came to the land of Gennesaret. When the men of that place recognized him, they sent into all that region round about, and brought to him all who were sick, and they begged him that they might only touch the fringe of his garment. As many as touched it were made whole.

— Matthew 14:34-36 WEB

SIGNS AND WONDERS

Jesus turned water into wine at the wedding at Cana:

This beginning of his signs Jesus did in Cana of Galilee, and revealed his glory; and his disciples believed in him.

— John 2:11 WEB

When they rowed about three or four miles, they saw Jesus approaching the boat, walking on the water; and they were frightened. But he said to them, "It is I; don't be afraid." Then they were willing to take him into the boat, and immediately the boat reached the shore where they were heading.

— John 6:19-21 NIV

JESUS CAME TO ...

Jesus speaking to Zacchaeus:

And Jesus said unto him, This day is salvation come to this house, forsomuch as he also is a son of Abraham. For the Son of man is come to seek and to save that which was lost.

— Luke 19:9-10 KJV

You know the message God sent to the people of Israel, announcing the good news of peace through Jesus Christ, who is Lord of all. You know what has happened throughout the province of Judea, beginning in Galilee after the baptism that John preached – how God anointed Jesus of Nazareth with the Holy Spirit and power, and how he went around doing good and healing all who were under the power of the devil, because God was with him.

— Acts 10:36-38 NIV

He who sins is of the devil, for the devil has been sinning from the beginning. To this end the Son of God was revealed, that he might destroy the works of the devil.

— 1 John 3:8 WEB

JESUS OUR ATTORNEY, OUR INTERCESSOR!!!

Who then is the one who condemns? No one. Christ Jesus, who died —more than that, who was raised to life—is at the right hand of God and is also interceding for us.

— Romans 8:34 NIV

My little children, I write these things to you so that you may not sin. If anyone sins, we have a Counselor with the Father, Jesus Christ, the righteous.

— 1 John 2:1 WEB

TESTIFY

A prayer testimony: I have detoured, derailed, and even jumped off the cliff a time or two as I have journeyed on the ever-narrowing road. God has been so good to me. The first prayer I remember having answered was when I was about seven years old. It is still very vivid in my mind. I had the mumps and was crying in pain. This was when only baby aspirin was available.

I remember my mother telling me to pray and ask Jesus to help me. I went to my room and quietly cried. I prayed and in just a few minutes the pain was gone. I remember going and telling my Mother with surprise and awe in my heart that He had answered my prayer. She affirmed and encouraged me that He always listens and answers. It's been over fifty years and if I try to remember I can still feel that bubbling up in my heart as it did then.

PAUSE AND PONDER

DO YOU PRAY DAILY? ARE YOU SPENDING TIME WITH HIM?

But seek ye first the kingdom of God, and his righteousness; and all these things shall be added unto you.

— Matthew 6:33 KJV

In these next verses, it reveals that Jesus took time to be alone with His Father in prayer. We must do the same.

And he withdrew himself into the wilderness, and prayed.

— Luke 5:16 KJV

And it came to pass in those days, that he went out into a mountain to pray, and continued all night in prayer to God.

— Luke 6:12 KJV

Who in the days of his flesh, having offered up prayers and petitions with strong crying and tears to him who was able to save him from death, and having been heard for his godly fear, though he was a Son, yet learned obedience by the things which he suffered; and having been made perfect, he became to all of those who obey him the author of eternal salvation named by God a high priest after the order of Melchizedek.

— Hebrews 5:7-10 WEB

A PRAYER YOU CAN PRAY

"Father help me to reverently submit and be obedient to Your will in my life. Help me to develop determination, discipline, and the ability to shut out all distractions as I spend time with You. In Jesus' name. Amen."

Lesson 10

Our Messiah And The Prophecies Foretold

Lesson Highlight:

> *For no prophecy ever came by the will of man: but holy*
> *men of God spoke, being moved by the Holy Spirit.*

> — 2 Peter 1:21 WEB

The Bible has a Big Picture, the picture of Messiah, Jesus Christ, and His wonderful plan for salvation. Redemption was woven through the books and verses from Genesis to Revelation by the Holy Spirit. The fact that these prophecies are of one mind, that of the Holy Spirit, and are in agreement with one another is incredible. This continuity that crosses many generations could only be accomplished supernaturally and by our Amazing Creator. He wants His people to know Him and what He is doing.

Receiving as the result of your faith the salvation of your souls. Concerning this salvation, the prophets who prophesied of the grace that should come to you have inquired and searched diligently, seeking the events and time the Spirit of Christ, who was within them, signified when He foretold the sufferings of Christ and the glories to follow. It was revealed to them that they were not serving themselves but you, concerning the things which are now reported to you by those who have preached the gospel to you through the Holy Spirit, who was sent from heaven—things into which the angels desire to look.

— 1 Peter 1:9-12 MEV

REVEALING

Remember the former things, those of long ago; I am God, and there is no other; I am God, and there is none like me. I make known the end from the beginning, from ancient times, what is still to come. I say: My purpose will stand, and I will do all that I please.

— Isaiah 46:9-10 NIV

A reference to David being a prophet:

Men and brethren, let me freely speak unto you of the patriarch David, that he is both dead and buried, and his sepulchre is with us unto this day. Therefore being a prophet, and knowing that God had sworn with an oath to him, that of the fruit of his loins, according to the flesh, he would raise up Christ to sit on his throne; He seeing this before spake of the resurrection of Christ, that his soul was not left in hell, neither his flesh did see corruption. This Jesus hath God raised up, whereof we all are witnesses.

— Acts 2:29-32 KJV

"Prophecy" defined by Merriam-Webster.com:

1. An inspired utterance of a prophet

2. The inspired declaration of divine will and purpose
3. A prediction of something to come.

THE WORD OF THE LORD

Moreover the word of the Lord came unto me, saying,

— Ezekiel 35:1 KJV

For God does speak—now one way, now another—though no one perceives it. In a dream, in a vision of the night, when deep sleep falls on people as they slumber in their beds, he may speak in their ears and terrify them with warnings.

— Job 33:14-16 NIV

The Revelation of Jesus Christ, which God gave unto him, to shew unto his servants things which must shortly come to pass; and he sent and signified it by his angel unto his servant John ...

— Revelation 1:1 KJV

PROPHECIES OF THE MESSIAH

There are a multitude of prophecies in the Old Testament that Jesus fulfilled. Some are very easily seen since we have the advantage of having the verses which reveal their fulfillment. Others are more difficult to perceive as though they have tracing paper covering them so that it causes you to strain to see.

As I searched the internet there was a wide range of the number of prophecies listed, from forty to four hundred. We will be looking at a few of these prophecies in this lesson.

As you move along through these scriptures I have written the Old Testament prophecies first. Immediately following are the verses that reveal the fulfillment from the New Testament. It is worth the invest-ment to purchase a good study Bible, investigate it thoroughly before buying one so you won't be disappointed. My study Bibles are all older and the translations are much different in some of the newer editions. Choose carefully.

THE APPOINTED TIME

But when the fulness of the time was come, God sent forth his Son, made of a woman, made under the law, to redeem them that were under the law, that we might receive the adoption of sons.

— Galatians 4:4-5 KJV

While we were yet in weakness [powerless to help ourselves], at the fitting time Christ died for (in behalf of) the ungodly. Now it is an extraordinary thing for one to give his life even for an upright man, though perhaps for a noble and lovable and generous benefactor someone might even dare to die. But God shows and clearly proves His [own] love for us by the fact that while we were still sinners, Christ (the Messiah, the Anointed One) died for us. Therefore, since we are now justified (acquitted, made righteous, and brought into right relationship with God) by Christ's blood, how much more [cer-tain is it that] we shall be saved by Him from the indignation and wrath of God.

— Romans 5:6-9 AMPC

Making known to us the mystery of His will, according to His good pleasure, which He purposed in Himself, as a plan for the fullness of time, to unite all things in Christ, which are in heaven and on earth.

— Ephesians 1:9-10 MEV

FORETOLD BY THE PROPHETS WITH FULFILLMENT VERSES

PROPHECY:

The LORD had said to Abram ..."I will bless those who bless you, and whoever curses you I will curse; and all peoples on earth will be blessed through you."

— Genesis 12:1a, 3 NIV

Fulfilled:

The book of the genealogy of Jesus Christ, the Son of David, the Son of Abraham ...

— Matthew 1:1 NKJV

PROPHECY:

Therefore the Lord himself shall give you a sign; Behold, a virgin shall conceive, and bear a son, and shall call his name Immanuel.

— Isaiah 7:14 KJV

Fulfilled:

Now the birth of Jesus Christ was like this; because when his mother, Mary, had been engaged to Joseph, before they came together, she was found pregnant by the Holy Spirit. Joseph, her husband, being a righteous man, and not willing to make her a public example, intended to put her away secretly. But when he thought about these things, behold, an angel of the Lord appeared to him in a dream, saying, "Joseph, son of David, don't be afraid to take to yourself Mary, your wife, for that which is conceived in her is of the Holy Spirit. She shall bring forth a son. You shall call his name JESUS, for it is he who shall save his people from their sins."Now all this has happened, that it might be fulfilled which was spoken by the Lord through the prophet, saying, "Behold, the virgin shall be with child, and shall bring forth a son. They shall call his name Immanuel;" which is, being interpreted, "God with us."

— Matthew 1:18-23 WEB

PROPHECY:

But thou, Bethlehem Ephratah, though thou be little among the thousands of Judah, yet out of thee shall he come forth unto me that is to be ruler in Israel; whose goings forth have been from of old, from everlasting.

— Micah 5:2 KJV

Fulfilled:

And Joseph also went up from Galilee, out of the city of Nazareth, into Judaea, unto the city of David, which is called Bethlehem; (because he was of the house and lineage of David:) To be taxed with Mary his espoused wife, being great with child. And so it was, that, while they were there, the days were accomplished that she should be delivered. And she brought forth her firstborn son, and wrapped him in swaddling clothes, and laid him in a manger; because there was no room for them in the inn.

— Luke 2:4-7 KJV

Hath not the scripture said, That Christ cometh of the seed of David, and out of the town of Bethlehem, where David was?

— John 7:42 KJV

PROPHECY:

Just as there were many who were appalled at him—his appearance was so disfigured beyond that of any human being and his form marred beyond human likeness—

— Isaiah 52:14 NIV

Fulfilled:

Then the soldiers of the governor took Jesus into the Praetorium and gathered the whole garrison around Him. And they stripped Him and put a scarlet robe on Him. When they had twisted a crown of thorns, they put it on His head, and a reed in His right hand. And they bowed the knee before Him and mocked Him, saying, "Hail, King of the Jews!" Then they spat on Him, and took the reed and struck Him on the head.

— Matthew 27:27-30 NKJV

PROPHECY:

Read the whole chapter when your time allows:

Who has believed our message and to whom has the arm of the Lord been revealed? He grew up before him like a tender shoot, and like a root out of dry ground. He had no beauty or majesty to attract us to him, nothing in his appearance that we should desire him.

—Isaiah 53:1-2 NIV

Fulfilled:

Even after Jesus had done performed so many signs in their presence, they still would not believe in him. This was to fulfill the word of Isaiah the prophet: "Lord, who has believed our message and to whom has the arm of the Lord been revealed?"

—John 12:37-38 NIV

But not all the Israelites accepted the good news. For Isaiah says, "Lord, who has believed our message?"

—Romans 10:16 NIV

PROPHECY:

He was despised and rejected by men, a man of sorrows, and acquainted with grief. and as one from whom men hide their faces he was despised, and we didn't respect him. Surely he has borne our infirmities, and carried our sorrows, yet we esteemed him stricken, struck by God, and afflicted. But he was wounded for our transgressions, he was bruised for our iniquities; the chastisement of our peace was on him, and with his stripes we are healed.

—Isaiah 53:3-5 WEB

Fulfilled:

When evening came, many who were demon-possessed were brought to him, and he drove out the spirits with a word and healed all the sick. This was to fulfill what was spoken through the prophet Isaiah: "He took up our infirmities and bore our diseases."

— Matthew 8:16-17 NIV

"He himself bore our sins" in his body on the cross, so that we might die to sins and live for righteousness; "by his wounds you have been healed."

— 1 Peter 2:24 NIV

Instead, one of the soldiers pierced Jesus' side with a spear, bringing a sudden flow of blood and water.

— John 19:34 NIV

PROPHECY:

We all, like sheep, have gone astray, each of us has turned to our own way; and the LORD has laid on him the iniquity of us all. He was oppressed and afflicted, yet he did not open his mouth; he was led like a lamb to the slaughter, and as a sheep before its shearers is silent, so he did not open his mouth.

— Isaiah 53:6-7 NIV

Fulfilled:

But Jesus made no reply, not even to a single charge—to the great amazement of the governor ... After they had mocked him, they took off the robe and put his own clothes on him. Then they led him away to crucify him.

— Matthew 27:14, 31 NIV

The next day John saw Jesus coming toward him and said, "Look, the Lamb of God, who takes away the sin of the world."

— John 1:29 MEV

Who was delivered for our offenses, and was raised again for our justification.

— Romans 4:25 KJV

PROPHECY:

Dogs have surrounded me; a band of evil men has encircled me, they have pierced my hands and my feet. I can count all my bones; people stare and gloat over me. They divide my garments among them and cast lots for my clothing.

— Psalm 22:16-18 EHV

Fulfilled:

The people stood watching, and the rulers even sneered at him. They said, "He saved others; let him save himself if he is God's Messiah, the Chosen One.

— Luke 23:35 NIV

These things happened so that the scripture would be fulfilled: "Not one of his bones will be broken," and, as another scripture says, "They will look on the one they have pierced."

— John 19:36-37 NIV

When they crucified Him, they divided His garments by casting lots to fulfill what was spoken by the prophet, "They divided My garments among themselves and for My clothing they cast lots." And sitting down, they kept watch over Him there.

— Matthew 27:35-36 MEV

PROPHECY:

They put gall in my food and gave me vinegar for my thirst.

— Psalm 69:21 NIV

Fulfilled:

Later, knowing that everything had now been finished, and so that Scripture would be fulfilled, Jesus said, "I am thirsty." A jar of wine vinegar was there, so they soaked a sponge in it, put the sponge on a stalk of the hyssop plant, and lifted it to Jesus lips. When he had received the drink, Jesus said, "It is finished." With that he bowed his head and gave up his spirit.

— John 19:28-30 NIV

PROPHECY:

He protects all his bones, not one of them will be broken.

— Psalm 34:20 NIV

Fulfilled:

These things happened so that the scripture would be fulfilled: "Not one of his bones will be broken," and, as another scripture says, "They will look on the one they have pierced.

— John 19:36-37 NIV

These prophecies were to teach and train the people the signs of the Savior's arrival (2 Peter 1:21). They declared the coming of the Messiah and should have helped the people recognize Christ Jesus, the One and Only. The Father was giving hope through these plans for the coming Savior of the world with the word spoken in advance.

It is undeniable that Jesus was the fulfillment of these prophecies (Romans 3:21-22). Even so, the leaders and people refused to believe, and sadly this unbelief continues today. This gross error with denial and rejection of Jesus was the fulfillment of these prophetic words also (Matthew 5:17). Our God truly is unfathomable, revealing the end from the beginning.

Declaring the end from the beginning, and from ancient times the things that are not yet done, saying, My counsel shall stand, and I will do all my pleasure

— Isaiah 46:10 KJV

PAUSE AND PONDER

DO YOU BELIEVE THAT GOD STILL SPEAKS TO HIS SERVANTS THE PROPHETS? HE SPEAKS ONE WAY AND THEN ANOTHER TO MAN IN DREAMS, IN A VISION?

Let's look at two of our previous verses:

For God may speak in one way, or in another, Yet man does not perceive it. In a dream, in a vision of the night, When deep sleep falls upon men, While slumbering on their beds, Then He opens the ears of men, And seals their instruction.

— Job 33:14-16 NKJV

Surely the Lord GOD does nothing without revealing His purpose to His servants the prophets.

— Amos 3:7 MEV

A PRAYER FOR YOU TO PRAY

"Oh Father, help my unbelief! Give me a keen ability to discern the true from the false. I ask You to help me incline my ear to hear You when You speak. Father make my heart tender and receptive to Your word in Jesus' name. Amen."

Lesson 11

Christ Crucifixion

Lesson Highlight:

> *Fixing our eyes on Jesus, the pioneer and perfecter of
>   faith. For the joy set before him he endured the cross,
>   scorning its shame, and sat down at the right hand of
>   the throne of God.*
>
> — Hebrews 12:2 NIV

There are no words to give us a clear understanding of the horrific nature of the crucifixion. How it must have felt for Jesus to walk through this suffering and abandonment since He fully knew what was to come. The emotions and pain His mother and others there with Him must have experienced as they witnessed Him fulfill the most masterfully planned event in all of history. What were the Father and all of heaven experiencing? Have you ever considered if you had been there would you have received or rejected the Son of God? That is something to ponder.

If you had been on the earth and witnessed all of these biblical accounts of the life of Jesus from the beginning to the end, how do you suppose it would have affected you? If you could have perceived the big picture, God's plan from the fall in the garden until all was "finished," how would you have reacted?

If your knowledge had included the prophets' declarations, angelic visitations, water into wine, walking on water, calming the storm, multiplying loaves and fishes...twice, healing the sick, raising the dead, casting out demons, betrayal, denial, trial, crucifixion, resurrection, ascension and the charge to "Go ye..." would you have accepted the invitation from Jesus to "follow me."

I would hope that we would all be burning ones for our Amazing Creator, even unto our death. We have the opportunity to accept, follow, and do it today. Embrace these accounts of the love of God and allow it to penetrate your heart. You must begin seeking Him, with your whole heart.

JESUS MADE THEM AWARE

> And Jesus going up to Jerusalem took the twelve disciples apart in the way, and said unto them, Behold, we go up to Jerusalem; and the Son of man shall be betrayed unto the chief priests and unto the scribes, and they shall condemn him to death, and shall deliver him to the Gentiles to mock, and to scourge, and to crucify him: and the third day he shall rise again.
>
> — Matthew 20:17-19 KJV

> And Jesus saith unto them, All ye shall be offended because of me this night: for it is written, I will smite the shepherd, and the sheep shall be scattered.
>
> — Mark 14:27 KJV

> Now when evening had come, he was reclining at the table with the twelve disciples. As they were eating, he said, "Most assuredly I tell

you, that one of you will betray me." They were exceedingly sorrowful, and each began to ask him, "It isn't me, is it, Lord?"

— Matthew 26:20-22 WEB

The Lord said, "Simon, Simon, behold, Satan asked to have you, that he might sift you as wheat, but I prayed for you, that your faith wouldn't fail. You, when once you have turned again, establish your brothers." He said to him, "Lord, I am ready to go with you both to prison and to death!" He said, "I tell you, Peter, the rooster will by no means crow today, before you deny that you know me three times."

— Luke 22:31-34 WEB

BETRAYAL AND JESUS ARRESTED

Men and brethren, this Scripture had to be fulfilled, which the Holy Spirit spoke before by the mouth of David concerning Judas, who became a guide to those who arrested Jesus.

— Acts 1:16 NKJV

While he was still speaking, behold, a multitude, and he who was called Judas, one of the twelve, went in front of them. He came near to Jesus to kiss him. But Jesus said to him, "Judas, do you betray the Son of Man with a kiss?" When those who were around him saw what was about to happen, they said to him, "Lord, shall we strike with the sword?" A certain one of them struck the servant of the high priest, and cut off his right ear. But Jesus answered, "Let me at least do this" -- and he touched his ear, and healed him. Jesus said to the chief priests, captains of the temple, and elders, who had come against him, "Have you come out as against a robber, with swords and clubs? When I was with you in the temple daily, you didn't stretch out your hands against me. But this is your hour, and the power of darkness." They seized him, and led him away, and brought him into the high priest's house. But Peter followed from a distance.

— Luke 22:47-54 WEB

But Peter said, "Man, I don't know what you are talking about!" Immediately, while he was still speaking, a rooster crowed. The Lord turned, and looked at Peter. Peter remembered the Lord's word, how he said to him, "Before the rooster crows you will deny me three times." He went out, and wept bitterly.

— Luke 22:60-62 WEB

THE PATH TO GOLGOTHA

For to this you were called, because Christ suffered for us, leaving us an example, that you should follow His steps: "He committed no sin, nor was deceit found in His mouth." When He was reviled, He did not revile back; when He suffered, He did not threaten, but He entrusted Himself to Him who judges righteously.

— 1 Peter 2:21-23 MEV

He went out, bearing his cross, to the place called "The place of a skull," which is called in Hebrew, "Golgotha,"

— John 19:17 WEB

As they came out, they found a man of Cyrene, Simon by name, and they compelled him to go with them, that he might carry his cross.

— Matthew 27:32 WEB

BECAUSE HE WAS NAILED TO A TREE

Christ purchased our freedom [redeeming us] from the curse (doom) of the Law [and its condemnation] by [Himself] becoming a curse for us, for it is written [in the Scriptures], Cursed is everyone who hangs on a tree (is crucified); to the end that through [their receiving] Christ Jesus, the blessing [promised] to Abraham might come upon the Gentiles, so that we through faith might [all] receive [the realization of] the promise of the [Holy] Spirit.

— Galatians 3:13-14 AMPC

The God of our fathers raised up Jesus, whom you killed, hanging him on a tree. God exalted him with his right hand to be a Prince and a Savior, to give repentance to Israel, and remission of sins.

— Acts 5:30-31 WEB

And you, being dead in your trespasses and the uncircumcision of your flesh, He has made alive together with Him, having forgiven you all trespasses, having wiped out the handwriting of requirements that was against us, which was contrary to us. And He has taken it out of the way, having nailed it to the cross. Having disarmed principalities and powers, He made a public spectacle of them, triumphing over them in it.

— Colossians 2:13-15 NKJV

Who his own self bare our sins in his own body on the tree, that we, being dead to sins, should live unto righteousness: by whose stripes ye were healed. For ye were as sheep going astray; but are now returned unto the Shepherd and Bishop of your souls.

— 1 Peter 2:24-25 KJV

CHRIST CRUCIFIED

It was the third hour, and they crucified him. The superscription of his accusation was written over him, "THE KING OF THE JEWS." With him they crucified two robbers; one on his right hand, and one on his left. The Scripture was fulfilled, which says, "He was numbered with transgressors." Those who passed by blasphemed him, wagging their heads, and saying,"Ha! You who destroy the temple, and build it in three days, save yourself, and come down from the cross!" Likewise, also the chief priests mocking among themselves with the scribes said, "He saved others. He can't save himself. Let the Christ, the King of Israel, now come down from the cross, that we may see and believe him." Those who were crucified with him reproached him.

— Mark 15:25-32 WEB

Then said Jesus, Father, forgive them; for they know not what they do. And they parted his raiment, and cast lots.

— Luke 23:34 KJV

And about the ninth hour Jesus cried with a loud voice, saying, E-li, E-li, la'-ma sa-bach'-tha-ni? That is to say, My God, my God, why hast thou forsaken me?

— Matthew 27:46 KJV

Near the cross of Jesus stood his mother, his mother's sister, Mary the wife of Clopas, and Mary Magdalene. When Jesus saw his mother there, and the disciple whom he loved standing nearby, he said to her, "Woman, here is your son," and to the disciple, "Here is your mother." From that time on, this disciple took her into his home.

— John 19:25-27 NIV

When Jesus therefore had received the vinegar, he said, It is finished: and he bowed his head, and gave up the ghost.

— John 19:30 KJV (Psalm 69:21)

It was now about the sixth hour (midday), and darkness enveloped the whole land and earth until the ninth hour (about three o'clock in the afternoon), while the sun's light faded or was darkened; and the curtain [of the Holy of Holies] of the temple was torn in two. And Jesus, crying out with a loud voice, said, Father, into Your hands I commit My spirit! And with these words, He expired.

— Luke 23:44-46 AMPC

Jesus, when he had cried again with a loud voice, yielded up the ghost. And, behold, the veil of the temple was rent in twain from the top to the bottom; and the earth did quake, and the rocks rent; and the graves were opened; and many bodies of the saints which slept arose, and came out of the graves after his resurrection, and went into the holy city, and appeared unto many. Now when the centurion, and they that were with him, watching Jesus, saw the earthquake, and those things that were done, they feared greatly, saying, Truly this was the Son of God. And many women were there beholding afar off, which followed Jesus from Galilee, ministering unto him.

— Matthew 27:50-55 KJV

ACCOMPLISHED THROUGH THE CROSS OF CHRIST JESUS

Looking to Jesus, the author and perfecter of faith, who for the joy that was set before him endured the cross, despising shame, and has sat down at the right hand of the throne of God.

— Hebrews 12:2 WEB

Because Christ also suffered for sins once, the righteous for the unrighteous, that he might bring you to God; being put to death in the flesh, but made alive in the spirit.

— 1 Peter 3:18 WEB

Therefore, having been justified by faith, we have peace with God through our Lord Jesus Christ, through whom also we have access by faith into this grace in which we stand, and rejoice in hope of the glory of God.

— Romans 5:1-2 NKJV

But because Jesus lives forever, he has a permanent priesthood. Therefore he is able to save completely those who come to God through him, because he always lives to intercede for them.

— Hebrews 7:24-25 NIV

And you, who were formerly alienated and enemies in your mind by wicked works, yet now He has reconciled in the body of His flesh through death, to present you holy and blameless and above reproach in His sight, if you continue in the faith, grounded and settled, and are not removed from the hope of the gospel, which you have heard, and which was preached to every creature which is under heaven, and of which I, Paul, have become a servant.

— Colossians 1:21-23 MEV

PAUSE AND PONDER

CAN YOU GRASP THE HORRIFIC NATURE OF THE CRUCIFIXION?

We must remember all that He has done for us. That is one reason communion is so important. It is a time to remember all that Jesus has done for us through His death on the cross.

> And he took bread, and gave thanks, and brake it, and gave unto them, saying, This is my body which is given for you: this do in remembrance of me. Likewise also the cup after supper, saying, This cup is the new testament in my blood, which is shed for you.

> — Luke 22:19-20 KJV

A PRAYER YOU CAN PRAY

"Lord help me to perceive what you went through and what you accomplished that made our redemption possible. Help me to grasp how it was planned from the beginning and that You came willingly and readily. In Your precious name, Jesus. Amen."

Jesus speaking:

> The reason my Father loves me is that I lay down my life— only to take it up again. No one takes it from me, but I lay it down of my own accord. I have authority to lay it down and authority to take it up again. This command I received from my Father."

> — John 10:17-18 NIV

Lesson 12

Burial And Resurrection

Lesson Highlight:

> *Or don't you know that all we who were baptized into*
> *Christ Jesus were baptized into his death? We were*
> *buried therefore with him through baptism to death,*
> *that just like Christ was raised from the dead*
> *through the glory of the Father, so we also might*
> *walk in newness of life. For if we have become*
> *united with him in the likeness of his death, we will*
> *also be part of his resurrection; knowing this, that*
> *our old man was crucified with him, that the body of*
> *sin might be done away with, so that we would no*
> *longer be in bondage to sin. For he who has died has*
> *been freed from sin. But if we died with Christ, we*
> *believe that we will also live with him; knowing that*
> *Christ, being raised from the dead, dies no more.*
> *Death no more has dominion over him! For the death*
> *that he died, he died to sin one time; but the life that*
> *he lives, he lives to God. Thus also consider your-*
> *selves also to be dead to sin, but alive to God in*

Christ Jesus our Lord. Therefore don't let sin reign in
your mortal body, that you should obey it in its lusts.

— Romans 6:3-12 WEB

UNDENIABLE

Jesus speaking to His disciples at the Last Supper:

> However when he, the Spirit of truth, has come, he will guide you
> into all the truth, for he will not speak from himself; but whatever
> things he hears, he will speak. He will declare to you the things that
> are to come.

— John 16:13 WEB

In the Book of Acts 2:25-28, the Apostle Peter gives an account of
and quotes Psalm 16:8-11 in which David prophecies about the coming
Messiah. Paul also quotes Psalm 16:10 in Acts 13:35. It is amazing the
consistency and fulfillment of biblical prophecies that run like a thread
throughout the Scriptures. The evidence of the truth and soundness of
the Word of God is undeniable, yet many deny it. Christianity is having
faith in God and His Word. Faith is believing.

Peter preaching on the day of Pentecost quoted Psalm 16:

> For David says concerning him, 'I saw the Lord always before my
> face, for he is on my right hand, that I should not be moved. There-
> fore my heart was glad, and my tongue rejoiced. Moreover my flesh
> also will dwell in hope; Because you will not leave my soul in Hades,
> Neither will you allow your Holy One to see decay. You made known
> to me the ways of life. You will make me full of gladness with your
> presence.

— Acts 2:25-28 WEB

BURIAL

When evening had come, there came a rich man from Arimathaea, named Joseph, who also himself was Jesus' disciple. This man went to Pilate, and asked for the body of Jesus. Then Pilate commanded the body to be given up. Joseph took the body, and wrapped it in a clean linen cloth, and laid it in his own new tomb, which he had hewn out in the rock, and he rolled a great stone to the door of the tomb, and departed. Mary Magdalene was there, and the other Mary, sitting opposite the tomb. Now on the next day, which is the day after the Preparation, the chief priests and the Pharisees were gathered together to Pilate, saying, "Sir, we remember what that deceiver said while he was still alive: 'After three days I will rise again.' Command therefore that the tomb be made secure until the third day, lest perhaps his disciples come at night and steal him away, and tell the people, 'He is risen from the dead;' and the last deception will be worse than the first." Pilate said to them, "You have a guard. Go, make it as secure as you can." So they went, and made the tomb secure, sealing the stone, the guard being with them.

— Matthew 27:57-66 WEB

RESURRECTION

Entering into the tomb, they saw a young man sitting on the right side, dressed in a white robe, and they were amazed. He said to them, "Don't be amazed. You seek Jesus, the Nazarene, who has been cruci-fied. He has risen. He is not here. Behold, the place where they laid him! But go, tell his disciples and Peter, 'He goes before you into Galilee. There you will see him, as he said to you.'" They went out, and fled from the tomb, for trembling and astonishment had come on them. They said nothing to anyone; for they were afraid.

— Mark 16:5-8 WEB

And they entered in, and found not the body of the Lord Jesus. And it came to pass, as they were much perplexed thereabout, behold, two men stood by them in shining garments: And as they were afraid, and bowed down their faces to the earth, they said unto them, Why seek ye the living among the dead? He is not here, but is risen: remember how he spake unto you when he was yet in Galilee, Saying, The Son of man must be delivered into the hands of sinful men, and be crucified, and the third day rise again.

— Luke 24:3-7 KJV

Now after the Sabbath, as it began to dawn on the first day of the week, Mary Magdalene and the other Mary came to see the tomb. Behold, there was a great earthquake, for an angel of the Lord descended from the sky, and came and rolled away the stone from the door, and sat on it. His appearance was like lightning, and his clothing white as snow. For fear of him, the guards shook, and became like dead men.

— Matthew 28:1-4 WEB

Peter preaching on the day of Pentecost:

"Fellow Israelites, listen to this: Jesus of Nazareth was a man accredited by God to you by miracles, wonders and signs, which God did among you through him, as you yourselves know. This man was handed over to you by God's deliberate plan and foreknowledge; and you, with the help of wicked men, put him to death by nailing him to the cross. But God raised him from the dead, freeing him from the agony of death, because it was impossible for death to keep its hold on him.

— Acts 2:22-24 NIV

... you killed the Creator of Life, whom God has raised from the dead, of which we are witnesses.

— Acts 3:15 MEV

For I delivered unto you first of all that which I also received, how that Christ died for our sins according to the scriptures; And that he was buried, and that he rose again the third day according to the scriptures: And that he was seen of Cephas, then of the twelve: After that, he was seen of above five hundred brethren at once; of whom the greater part remain unto this present, but some are fallen asleep. After that, he was seen of James; then of all the apostles. And last of all he was seen of me also, as of one born out of due time.

— 1 Corinthians 15:3-8 KJV

In the former account [which I prepared], O Theophilus, I made [a continuous report] dealing with all the things which Jesus began to do and to teach, until the day when He ascended, after He through the Holy Spirit had instructed and commanded the apostles (special messengers) whom He had chosen. To them also He showed Himself alive after His passion (His suffering in the garden and on the cross) by [a series of] many convincing demonstrations [unquestionable evidences and infallible proofs], appearing to them during forty days and talking [to them] about the things of the kingdom of God.

— Acts 1:1-3 AMPC

JESUS: FIRSTBORN FROM THE DEAD

Let us look to Jesus, the author and finisher of our faith, who for the joy that was set before Him endured the cross, despising the shame, and is seated at the right hand of the throne of God. For consider Him who endured such hostility from sinners against Himself, lest you become weary and your hearts give up.

— Hebrews 12:2-3 MEV

And we are witnesses of all things which He did both in the land of the Jews and in Jerusalem, whom they killed by hanging on a tree. Him God raised up on the third day, and showed Him openly, not to all the people, but to witnesses chosen before by God, even to us who ate and drank with Him after He arose from the dead.

— Acts 10:39-41 NKJV

And from Jesus Christ, who is the faithful witness, and the first begotten of the dead, and the prince of the kings of the earth. Unto him that loved us, and washed us from our sins in his own blood, and hath made us kings and priests unto God and his Father; to him be glory and dominion for ever and ever. Amen.

— Revelation 1:5-6 KJV

FOLLOW AND GO

Thus says Yahweh, your Redeemer, the Holy One of Israel: I am Yahweh your God, who teaches you to profit, who leads you by the way that you should go.

— Isaiah 48:17 WEB

For it has been granted to you on behalf of Christ not only to believe in him, but also to suffer for him, since you are going through the same struggle you saw I had, and now hear that I still have.

— Philippians 1:29-30 NIV

For what glory is it, if, when you sin, you patiently endure beating? But if, when you do well, you patiently endure suffering, this is commendable with God. For to this were you called, because Christ also suffered for us, leaving us an example, that you should follow his steps,

— 1 Peter 2:20-21 WEB

I am crucified with Christ: nevertheless I live; yet not I, but Christ liveth in me: and the life which I now live in the flesh I live by the faith of the Son of God, who loved me, and gave himself for me.

— Galatians 2:20 KJV

Establishing and strengthening the souls and the hearts of the disciples, urging and warning and encouraging them to stand firm in the faith, and [telling them] that it is through many hardships and tribulations we must enter the kingdom of God.

— Acts 14:22 AMPC

Therefore, since Christ suffered for us in the flesh, arm yourselves also with the same mind, for he who has suffered in the flesh has ceased from sin, that he no longer should live the rest of his time in the flesh for the lusts of men, but for the will of God. For we have spent enough of our past lifetime in doing the will of the Gentiles-- when we walked in lewdness, lusts, drunkenness, revelries, drinking parties, and abominable idolatries ... Beloved, do not think it strange concerning the fiery trial which is to try you, as though some strange thing happened to you; but rejoice to the extent that you partake of Christ's sufferings, that when His glory is revealed, you may also be glad with exceeding joy.

— 1 Peter 4:1-3, 12-13 NKJV

And He said to them, Go into all the world and preach and publish openly the good news (the Gospel) to every creature [of the whole human race]. He who believes [who adheres to and trusts in and relies on the Gospel and Him Whom it sets forth] and is baptized will be saved [from the penalty of eternal death]; but he who does not believe [who does not adhere to and trust in and rely on the Gospel and Him Whom it sets forth] will be condemned. And these attesting signs will accompany those who believe: in My name they will drive out demons; they will speak in new languages; they will pick up serpents; and [even] if they drink anything deadly, it will not hurt them; they will lay their hands on the sick, and they will get well.

— Mark 16:15-18 AMPC

EAGER TO SHARE

After being filled with the Holy Spirit I was burning to tell others about the love of Jesus. I had great liberty to do so with my employer at the time and was able to share with anyone encountered through work who seemed receptive. I wanted to do more but going alone from house to house was not an option. Creativity struck! My children and I placed cards with the plan of salvation and a poem about Jesus in plastic sandwich bags.

On several occasions, we would venture to one of the local bars in the very early evening placing them on windshields in the parking lot. If I remember correctly we never saw anyone in the parking lots while there. There was never a problem as we did this and it was great fun. In times past I have found small salvation leaflets on benches at the zoo, on public bathroom counters, on mirrors, and even slipped into rolls of toilet paper.

Through the years as I have shared Jesus with others I have been very fortunate with only a few rejecting to hear the message. There have been some people who with great anger refused prayer as well. I felt their rejection revealed deep wounds inflicted by the church or by those who professed Christianity. Most are grateful for prayer but I do live in the Bible Belt and that makes a big difference.

Whatever you do, be a person of integrity and honor others in your efforts. Most importantly: HONOR GOD!

FINAL INSTRUCTIONS ON HOW TO LIVE

Jesus speaking to His disciples:

> "Let your waist be girded and your lights be burning, and you be like men waiting for their master to return from the wedding banquet, so that they may open the door immediately for him when he comes and knocks. Blessed are those servants whom the master will find watching when he comes. Truly I say to you, he will dress himself and have them sit down to dine, and he will come and serve them. If he comes in the second watch, or comes in the third watch, and finds them so, blessed are those servants ...Therefore be ready, for the Son of Man is coming at an hour you do not expect."
>
> — Luke 12:35-38, 40 MEV

But the end of all things is near. Therefore be of sound mind, self-controlled, and sober in prayer. And above all things be earnest in your love among yourselves, for love covers a multitude of sins. Be hospitable one to another without grumbling. According as each has received a gift, be ministering it among yourselves, as good stewards of the grace of God in its various forms. If any man speaks, let it be as it were oracles of God. If any man serves, let it be as of the strength which God supplies, that in all things God may be glorified through

Jesus Christ, to whom belong the glory and the dominion forever and ever. Amen.

— 1 Peter 4:7-11 WEB

Jesus speaking to His disciples:

"Therefore keep watch, because you do not know on what day your Lord will come ... So you also must be ready, because the Son of Man will come at an hour when you do not expect him.

— Matthew 24:42, 44 NIV

PAUSE & PONDER

WHAT ABOUT YOU? DO YOU SHARE THE LOVE OF JESUS WITH OTHERS THROUGH DEEDS? ARE YOU SHARING THE GOSPEL? ARE YOU SNATCHING OTHERS FROM THE FIRE?

Keep yourselves in the love of God, looking for the mercy of our Lord Jesus Christ to eternal life. On some have compassion, making a distinction, and some save, snatching them out of the fire with fear, hating even the clothing stained by the flesh.

— Jude 1:21-23 WEB

Ask the Lord what you can do and He will show you. Start small and build from there. Be smart and be careful. Remember giving a smile, a kind word, and a prayer are huge to someone who needs it. Be creative!!! Everyone needs our precious Jesus as their Lord and Savior.

Then he said to his disciples, "The harvest indeed is plentiful, but the laborers are few. Pray therefore that the Lord of the harvest will send forth laborers into his harvest."

— Matthew 9:37-38 WEB

A PRAYER YOU CAN PRAY

"Oh Lord of the harvest send out workers into the harvest fields around the earth. Send them into the dark places and let their blazing lights shine forth to draw men, women, and children unto you!!! Let gifts and callings come forth with the evidence of miracles, signs, and wonders in Jesus' Name! Amen."

Lesson 13

God The Holy Spirit

Lesson Highlight:

> *So then, those who are in the flesh cannot please God.
> But you are not in the flesh but in the Spirit, if
> indeed the Spirit of God dwells in you. Now if
> anyone does not have the Spirit of Christ, he is not
> His. And if Christ is in you, the body is dead because
> of sin, but the Spirit is life because of righteousness.
> But if the Spirit of Him who raised Jesus from the
> dead dwells in you, He who raised Christ from the
> dead will also give life to your mortal bodies through
> His Spirit who dwells in you.*

> — Romans 8:8-11 NKJV

THE GIFT OF HOLY SPIRIT

Therefore tell the house of Israel, Thus says the Lord Yahweh ... A
new heart also will I give you, and a new spirit will I put within you;

and I will take away the stony heart out of your flesh, and I will give you a heart of flesh. I will put my Spirit within you, and cause you to walk in my statutes, and you shall keep my ordinances, and do them.

— Ezekiel 36:22a, 26-27 WEB

Jesus said to his disciples:

If ye then, being evil, know how to give good gifts unto your children: how much more shall your heavenly Father give the Holy Spirit to them that ask him?

— Luke 11:13 KJV

Peter said to them, "Repent, and be baptized, everyone of you, in the name of Jesus Christ for the forgiveness of sins, and you will receive the gift of the Holy Spirit. For to you is the promise, and to your children, and to all who are far off, even as many as the Lord our God will call to himself."

— Acts 2:38-39 WEB

How shall we escape if we ignore so great a salvation? This salvation, which was first announced by the Lord, was confirmed to us by those who heard him. God also testified to it by signs, wonders and various miracles, and by gifts of the Holy Spirit distributed according to his will.

— Hebrews 2:3-4 NIV

OUR COUNSELOR, THE SPIRIT OF TRUTH

Jesus speaking about Holy Spirit at the Lord's Supper:

The Spirit of truth, whom the world can't receive; for it doesn't see him, neither knows him. You know him, for he lives with you, and will be in you. I will not leave you orphans. I will come to you ... But the Counselor, the Holy Spirit, whom the Father will send in my name, he will teach you all things, and bring to your memory all that I said to you.

— John 14:17-18, 26 WEB

Jesus speaking to the disciples at the Lord's Supper:

Nevertheless I tell you the truth: It is to your advantage that I go away, for if I don't go away, the Counselor won't come to you. But if I go, I will send him to you. When he has come, he will convict the world in respect to sin, and righteousness, and judgment; of sin, because they don't believe in me; of righteousness, because I am going to my Father, and you see me no more; of judgment, because the prince of this world has been judged ... However when he, the Spirit of truth, has come, he will guide you into all the truth, for he will not speak from himself; but whatever things he hears, he will speak. He will declare to you the things that are to come.

— John 16:7-11, 13 WEB

BAPTIZED WITH THE HOLY SPIRIT—> THE SPIRIT OF GOD'S SON

John answered, saying to all, "I indeed baptize you with water; but One mightier than I is coming, whose sandal strap I am not worthy to loose. He will baptize you with the Holy Spirit and fire.

— Luke 3:16 NKJV

Jesus speaking to the disciples after the resurrection:

> For John baptized with water, but you shall be baptized with the Holy Spirit not many days from now; But you shall receive power when the Holy Spirit comes upon you. And you shall be My witnesses in Jerusalem, and in all Judea and Samaria, and to the ends of the earth.

> — Acts 1:5, 8 MEV

> And when the day of Pentecost was fully come, they were all with one accord in one place. And suddenly there came a sound from heaven as of a rushing mighty wind, and it filled all the house where they were sitting. And there appeared unto them cloven tongues like as of fire, and it sat upon each of them. And they were all filled with the Holy Ghost, and began to speak with other tongues, as the Spirit gave them utterance.

> — Acts 2:1-4 KJV

> And because you are sons, God sent forth the Spirit of his Son into your hearts, crying, "Abba, Father!" So you are no longer a bondservant, but a son; and if a son, then an heir of God through Christ.

> — Galatians 4:6-7 WEB

> For I know that through your prayer and the support of the Spirit of Jesus Christ, this will result in my deliverance.

> — Philippians 1:19 MEV

> And Paul and Silas passed through the territory of Phrygia and Galatia, having been forbidden by the Holy Spirit to proclaim the Word in [the province of] Asia. And when they had come opposite Mysia,

they tried to go into Bithynia, but the Spirit of Jesus did not permit them.

— Acts 16:6-7 AMPC

MY EXPERIENCE

I was raised Baptist and was saved at the age of 7 years old. My parents were keenly aware that the most important decision for every person is where they will spend eternity. They taught us and nurtured our faith in God. My father led me to Jesus as my personal Lord and Savior and I am so very grateful.

In late November 1995, I went with a friend to the Brownsville Revival. As I observed the power of the presence of the Holy Spirit I understood it was very real but wasn't sure if it was for me. I received prayer from the prayer team and could feel a stirring within me.

Evangelist Steve Hill and Pastor John Kilpatrick worked their way through the crowd praying for people. As Pastor Kilpatrick got close to me he merely reached toward me to pray and I received the baptism of the Holy Spirit. He never touched me. I was filled with joy unspeakable.

I was forever changed in that instant and I am so very thankful. When I got home I realized my Bible had come alive. The words were jumping off the pages. My understanding had greatly increased and I could not read it enough.

WE ARE HIS TEMPLE AND ARE SEALED WITH HOLY SPIRIT

Do you not know that your body is the temple (the very sanctuary) of the Holy Spirit Who lives within you, Whom you have received [as a Gift] from God? You are not your own, you were bought with a price [purchased with a preciousness and paid for, made His own]. So then, honor God and bring glory to Him in your body.

— 1 Corinthians 6:19-20 AMPC

And what agreement has the temple of God with idols? For you are the temple of the living God. As God has said: "I will dwell in them And walk among them. I will be their God, And they shall be My people."

— 2 Corinthians 6:16 NKJV

In whom you also, having heard the word of the truth, the gospel of your salvation, -- in whom, having also believed, you were sealed with the Holy Spirit of promise, who is a pledge of our inheritance, to the redemption of God's own possession, to the praise of his glory.

— Ephesians 1:13-14 WEB

Now it is God who makes both us and you stand firm in Christ. He anointed us, set his seal of ownership on us, and put his Spirit in our hearts as a deposit, guaranteeing what is to come.

— 2 Corinthians 1:21-22 NIV

Don't grieve the Holy Spirit of God, in whom you were sealed to the day of redemption.

— Ephesians 4:30 WEB

FREEDOM

There is therefore now no condemnation to them which are in Christ Jesus, who walk not after the flesh, but after the Spirit. For the law of the Spirit of life in Christ Jesus hath made me free from the law of sin and death.

— Romans 8:1-2 KJV

But thanks be to God, for you were slaves of sin, but you have obeyed from the heart that form of teaching to which you were entrusted, and having been freed from sin, you became the slaves of right-eousness.

— Romans 6:17-18 MEV

Jesus therefore said to those Jews who had believed him, "If you remain in my word, then you are truly my disciples. You will know the truth, and the truth will make you free ... If therefore the Son makes you free, you will be free indeed.

— John 8:31-32, 36 WEB

Now the Lord is the Spirit, and where the Spirit of the Lord is, there is freedom.

— 2 Corinthians 3:17 NIV

TESTIMONY:

This is the best way I can explain myself spiritually before and after the baptism of the Holy Spirit. Before I felt like I had a glass of clean cool water but after receiving the Holy Spirit it was like jumping into an ocean of this clean cool water that was fully refreshing. Going from a few sips to total immersion. Yes, joy unspeakable!

Another thought I have had through the years was before the baptism it was like communicating to God with two tin cans connected by a string, although I did not perceive it. After receiving the baptism of the Holy Spirit it was like having a super-high-speed internet connection to God.

That was not the only connection that occurred. There was also a direct connection to other Spirit-filled believers. These divine connections are truly amazing. I am not sure but perhaps they are specifically to those with like assignments or those with whom there are future, shared assignments. I can explain it as being a joyful reunion with someone which you do not know.

It feels like seeing your long-lost friend that you love. The reality is you hardly know or perhaps have never met them before. A direct connection at a spiritual level. Our Heavenly Father is so much fun!

One other thing that is awesome and extremely beneficial is having "a knowing in your knower." Sometimes you just know things. A good rule of thumb is that you should always pray about "those things you just know." Thank You Father for sending the Holy Spirit!!! We are forever grateful.

PAUSE & PONDER

ARE YOU WILLING TO RECEIVE THE BAPTISM OF THE HOLY SPIRIT?

It forever changed me and it will change you too. Be willing and go after the wonderful gift of Holy Spirit. Run in hot pursuit and open your heart to receive Him.

Jesus said:

> But you shall receive power when the Holy Spirit comes upon you. And you shall be My witnesses in Jerusalem, and in all Judea and Samaria, and to the ends of the earth.
>
> — Acts 1:8 MEV

> And Peter answered them, Repent (change your views and purpose to accept the will of God in your inner selves instead of rejecting it) and be baptized, every one of you, in the name of Jesus Christ for the forgiveness of and release from your sins; and you shall receive the gift of the Holy Spirit.
>
> — Acts 2:38 AMPC

A PRAYER YOU CAN PRAY

"Dear God, I repent for my sins and stubbornness as I try to go my own way. Forgive me and help me to be obedient and submissive to You. I ask to be filled to overflow daily with Your Holy Spirit in Jesus' name. Amen."

Lesson 14

Holy Spirit...Our Helper

Lesson Highlight:

> *However when he, the Spirit of truth, has come, he will guide you into all the truth, for he will not speak from himself; but whatever things he hears, he will speak. He will declare to you the things that are to come.*

— John 16:13 WEB

Ephesians 4:30 tells us not to grieve the Holy Spirit and in 1 Thessalonians 5:19, we are instructed not to quench the Spirit. We are on His team and He is on ours so we must be sensitive to His promptings. We should strive to grow in this area. For me most of these prompts are subtle, like a gentle whisper. I have purposed in my heart to keep in tune as I continue to learn to walk by the leading of the Holy Spirit (Galatians 5:16).

I was 22 years old and driving to nursing school when suddenly I was overwhelmed with a heavy burden. As I processed the feeling of something being wrong, I decided to turn around and go back home, thinking perhaps the Holy Spirit's prompting was protecting me from a possible wreck or something. Cutting class for the day was not good, especially without having something tangible to put my finger on.

My two-year-old daughter was with my parents for the day, as she always was. I am very thankful for their help or I would have never made it through school. My Dad was very surprised at my return having been gone only minutes. As I explained what had happened he affirmed and encouraged my decision. He advised me to never resist these promptings but to recognize it as the leading of the Holy Spirit and always yield.

UNDERSTANDING HOLY SPIRIT

The first three passages are Jesus speaking to his disciples at the Last Supper.

> And I will pray the Father, and he shall give you another Comforter, that he may abide with you for ever.
>
> — John 14:16 KJV

> But when the Comforter is come, whom I will send unto you from the Father, even the Spirit of truth, which proceedeth from the Father, he shall testify of me.
>
> — John 15:26 KJV

> He will glorify me, for he will take from what is mine, and will declare it to you. All things whatever the Father has are mine; therefore I said that he takes of mine, and will declare it to you.
>
> — John 16:14-15 WEB

> But you are not in the flesh but in the Spirit, if it is so that the Spirit of God dwells in you. But if any man doesn't have the Spirit of Christ,

he is not his. If Christ is in you, the body is dead because of sin, but the spirit is alive because of righteousness. But if the Spirit of him who raised up Jesus from the dead dwells in you, he who raised up Christ Jesus from the dead will also give life to your mortal bodies through his Spirit who dwells in you ... For you didn't receive the spirit of bondage again to fear, but you received the spirit of adoption, whereby we cry, "Abba! Father!"

— Romans 8:9-11,15 WEB

Be eager and strive earnestly to guard and keep the harmony and oneness of [and produced by] the Spirit in the binding power of peace. [There is] one body and one Spirit—just as there is also one hope [that belongs] to the calling you received.

— Ephesians 4:3-4 AMPC

BE THE TEMPLE

Don't you know that you are a temple of God, and that God's Spirit lives in you? If anyone destroys the temple of God, God will destroy him; for God's temple is holy, which you are.

— 1 Corinthians 3:16-17 WEB

So then you are no longer strangers and sojourners, but you are fellow citizens with the saints, and of the household of God, being built on the foundation of the apostles and prophets, Christ Jesus himself being the chief cornerstone; in whom the whole building, fitted together, grows into a holy temple in the Lord; in whom you also are built together for a habitation of God in the Spirit.

— Ephesians 2:19-22 WEB

You also, as living stones, are built up as a spiritual house, to be a holy priesthood, to offer up spiritual sacrifices, acceptable to God through Jesus Christ.

— 1 Peter 2:5 WEB

OUR HEARTS

Now hope does not disappoint, because the love of God has been poured out in our hearts by the Holy Spirit who was given to us.

— Romans 5:5 NKJV

... who also has sealed us and given us the Spirit in our hearts as a guarantee.

— 2 Corinthians 1:22 NKJV

Likewise, the Spirit helps us in our weaknesses, for we do not know what to pray for as we ought, but the Spirit Himself intercedes for us with groanings too deep for words. He who searches the hearts knows what the mind of the Spirit is, because He intercedes for the saints according to the will of God.

— Romans 8:26-27 MEV

I pray these verses for myself daily:

I pray that out of his glorious riches he may strengthen you with power through his Spirit in your inner being, so that Christ may dwell in your hearts through faith. And I pray that you, being rooted and established in love, may have power, together with all the Lord's Holy people, to grasp how wide and long and high and deep is the love of Christ, and to know this love that surpasses knowledge—that you may be filled to the measure of all the fullness of God. Now to him who is able to do immeasurably more than all we ask or imagine, according to his power that is at work within us, to him be glory in the church and in Christ Jesus throughout all generations, for ever and ever! Amen.

— Ephesians 3:16-21 NIV

HE TEACHES, WARNS & FELLOWSHIPS WITH US

But the Counselor, the Holy Spirit, whom the Father will send in my name, he will teach you all things, and bring to your memory all that I said to you.

— John 14:26 WEB

Jesus speaking:

"When you are brought before synagogues, rulers and authorities, do not worry about how you will defend yourselves, or what you will say, for the Holy Spirit will teach you at that time what you should say."

— Luke 12:11-12 NIV

Now, behold, I go bound by the Spirit to Jerusalem, not knowing what will happen to me there; except that the Holy Spirit testifies in every city, saying that bonds and afflictions wait for me.

— Acts 20:22-23 WEB

The grace (favor and spiritual blessing) of the Lord Jesus Christ and the love of God and the presence and fellowship (the communion and sharing together, and participation) in the Holy Spirit be with you all. Amen (so be it).

— 2 Corinthians 13:14 AMPC

HOLY SPIRIT IN ACTION

And the earth was without form, and void; and darkness was upon the face of the deep. And the Spirit of God moved upon the face of the waters.

— Genesis 1:2 KJV

Of Otheniel a judge of Israel:

And when the children of Israel cried unto the LORD, the LORD raised up a deliverer to the children of Israel, who delivered them, even Othniel the son of Kenaz, Caleb's younger brother. And the Spirit of the LORD came upon him, and he judged Israel, and went out to war: and the LORD delivered Chushanrishathaim king of Mesopotamia into his hand; and his hand prevailed against Chushan-rishathaim.

— Judges 3:9-10 KJV

Speaking of Samson:

Then went Samson down, and his father and his mother, to Timnath, and came to the vineyards of Timnath: and, behold, a young lion roared against him. And the Spirit of the LORD came mightily upon him, and he rent him as he would have rent a kid, and he had nothing in his hand: but he told not his father or his mother what he had done.

— Judges 14:5-6 KJV

But when he thought about these things, behold, an angel of the Lord appeared to him in a dream, saying, "Joseph, son of David, don't be afraid to take to yourself Mary, your wife, for that which is conceived in her is of the Holy Spirit. She shall bring forth a son. You shall call his name JESUS, for it is he who shall save his people from their sins."

— Matthew 1:20-21 WEB

Then was Jesus led up of the Spirit into the wilderness to be tempted of the devil.

— Matthew 4:1 KJV

Then the Spirit said to Philip, "Go near and overtake this chariot." So Philip ran to him, and heard him reading the prophet Isaiah, and said, "Do you understand what you are reading?" And he said, "How can I, unless someone guides me?" And he asked Philip to come up and sit with him.

— Acts 8:29-31 NKJV

... by the power of signs and wonders, by the power of the Spirit of God, so that from Jerusalem and as far around as Illyricum, I have fully preached the gospel of Christ.

— Romans 15:19 MEV

For Christ also suffered once for sins, the righteous for the unrighteous, to bring you to God. He was put to death in the body but made alive in the Spirit.

— 1 Peter 3:18 NIV

But if the Spirit of Him who raised Jesus from the dead lives in you, He who raised Christ from the dead will also give life to your mortal bodies through His Spirit that lives in you. Therefore, brothers, we are debtors not to the flesh, to live according to the flesh. For if you live according to the flesh, you will die, but if through the Spirit you put to death the deeds of the body, you will live.

— Romans 8:11-13 MEV

TESTIFY

During my nursing career, I spent many years caring for people and sharing the gospel with others as opportunity allowed. About 20 years ago, I was about to approach a person to share the Gospel, this is what I felt in my spirit. I felt like I was at a wide-open run with full intent and boldness to share the gospel when the Holy Spirit reined me in. It was a firm steady feeling of being restrained. I felt it so strong in my spirit that it seemed physical. I was very surprised since this had never happened before and hasn't happened since. I thought it was very odd but I was obedient to this restraint.

This person seemed pleasant and nice at first, but as the shift progressed there was anger and verbal abuse. It increased as the night wore on. I was rather unclear and puzzled about the incident. After much thought and prayer, I felt it was the Lord's protection. I am very grateful.

Learn to be quick to yield to the Holy Spirit's subtle prompting, you can be sure it is for your good. The more you yield the better you become at perceiving these promptings. The more you ignore and blow them off the less sensitive you become and your spirit man will grow dull. One of the things I pray for myself is: "Lord help me to be spontaneously obedient when you speak." This has been a process for me and is an ongoing one.

PAUSE & PONDER

HAVE YOU EVER HEARD HOLY SPIRIT SPEAKING?

When you got saved you were sealed with Holy Spirit (Ephesians

1:13-14; 2 Corinthians 1:21-22). Understand it is necessary to listen for His whispers and subtle promptings (Isaiah 55:3; Revelation 3:22).

YOU MUST LEARN TO LISTEN - NOT ONLY HEAR WITH YOUR EARS BUT WITH YOUR HEART.

But they did not listen or incline their ear to turn from their wickedness, to burn no incense to other gods.

— Jeremiah 44:5 NKJV

And the Lord has sent to you all His servants the prophets, rising early and sending them, but you have not listened nor inclined your ear to hear.

— Jeremiah 25:4 NKJV

A prayer verse:

For this people's heart has grown callous. Their ears are dull of hearing. Their eyes they have closed. Lest they should see with their eyes, Hear with their ears, Understand with their heart, Would turn again, And I would heal them.

— Acts 28:27 WEB

A PRAYER YOU CAN PRAY

"Holy Spirit remove from me any dullness of understanding, give me eyes to see and ears to hear and a teachable heart to understand what You are saying. In Jesus name. Amen."

Lesson 15

Gifts Of The Holy Spirit

Lesson Highlight:

> *For the gifts and calling of God are without repentance.*
>
> — Romans 11:29 KJV

> *For God's gifts and His call are irrevocable. [He never withdraws them when once they are given, and He does not change His mind about those to whom He gives His grace or to whom He sends His call.]*
>
> — Romans 11:29 AMPC

I have previously advised that you always take any teaching or instruction to the Bible for clarification and understanding. The gifts of the Holy Spirit are very controversial for many, so once again I encourage you to take it to the Word of God. Seek the Lord in this area through prayer as well. Let's look at what Jesus said and notice in verse 16 Jesus says regarding the Holy Spirit: "...be with you forever." Forever includes now. In verse 17 "...the world can't receive him..."

. . .

Jesus speaking about the Holy Spirit at the Lord's Supper:

> If you love me, keep my commandments. I will pray to the Father, and he will give you another Counselor, that he may be with you forever, -- the Spirit of truth, whom the world can't receive; for it doesn't see him, nor knows him. You know him, for he lives with you, and will be in you. I will not leave you orphans. I will come to you ... But the Counselor, the Holy Spirit, whom the Father will send in my name, he will teach you all things, and bring to your memory all that I said to you.

— John 14:15-18, 26 WEB

SPIRITUAL GIFTS TAKEN FROM:

1 Corinthians 12:8-10 KJV
    Word of Wisdom
    Word of Knowledge
    Faith
    Gift of Healing
    Working of Miracles
    Prophecy
    Discerning of spirits
    Speaking in Tongues
    Interpretation of Tongues

"Gift" defined by Merriam-Webster.com:

1. a notable capacity, talent, or endowment
2. something voluntarily transferred by one person to another without compensation
3. the act, right, or power of giving

SPIRITUAL FATHER TO HIS SON

Notice in the following verse that the Apostle Paul calls Timothy his true son in the faith. The following verses are a father, the Apostle Paul, giving instructions to his beloved son, Timothy.

Paul, an apostle of Jesus Christ by the commandment of God our Saviour, and Lord Jesus Christ, which is our hope; Unto Timothy, my own son in the faith: Grace, mercy, and peace, from God our Father and Jesus Christ our Lord.

— 1 Timothy 1:1-2 KJV

Don't neglect the gift that is in you, which was given to you by prophecy, with the laying on of the hands of the elders.

— 1 Timothy 4:14 WEB

For this cause, I remind you that you should stir up the gift of God which is in you through the laying on of my hands. For God didn't give us a spirit of fear, but of power and love and discipline.

— 2 Timothy 1:6-7 WEB

HOLY SPIRIT, A GIFT FROM THE FATHER

To these he also shown himself alive after his suffering by many proofs, appearing to them over a period of forty days, and spoke about God's kingdom. Being assembled together with them, he charged them, "Don't depart from Jerusalem, but wait for the promise of the Father, which you heard from me.

— Acts 1:3-4 WEB

Then Peter said unto them, Repent, and be baptized every one of you in the name of Jesus Christ for the remission of sins, and ye shall receive the gift of the Holy Ghost. For the promise is unto you, and to your children, and to all that are afar off, even as many as the Lord our God shall call.

— Acts 2:38-39 KJV

HOLY SPIRIT: THE GIFT THAT GIVES GIFTS

But to each one of us was the grace given according to the measure of the gift of Christ. Therefore he says, "When he ascended on high, he led captivity captive, and gave gifts to men.

— Ephesians 4:7-8 WEB

If you then, evil as you are, know how to give good gifts [gifts that are to their advantage] to your children, how much more will your heavenly Father give the Holy Spirit to those who ask and continue to ask Him!

— Luke 11:13 AMPC

How will we escape, if we neglect so great a salvation -- which at the first having been spoken through the Lord, was confirmed to us by those who heard; God also bearing witness with them, both by signs and wonders, and by various works of power, and by gifts of the Holy Spirit, according to his own will?

— Hebrews 2:3-4 WEB

FOR THE COMMON GOOD

Now concerning spiritual gifts, brothers, I don't want you to be ignorant ... Now there are various kinds of gifts, but the same Spirit ... But to each one is given the manifestation of the Spirit for the profit of all. For to one is given through the Spirit the word of wisdom, and to another the word of knowledge, according to the same Spirit; to another faith, by the same Spirit; and to another gifts of healings, by the same Spirit; and to another workings of miracles; and to another prophecy; and to another discerning of spirits; to another different kinds of languages; and to another the interpretation of languages. But the one and the same Spirit works all of these, distributing to each one separately as he desires.

— 1 Corinthians 12:1, 4, 7-11 WEB

EAGERLY DESIRE SPIRITUAL GIFTS

Now you are the body of Christ, and members individually. And God has appointed these in the church: first apostles, second prophets, third teachers, after that miracles, then gifts of healings, helps, administrations, varieties of tongues. Are all apostles? Are all prophets? Are all teachers? Are all workers of miracles? Do all have gifts of healings? Do all speak with tongues? Do all interpret? But earnestly desire the best gifts.

— 1 Corinthians 12:27-31a NKJV

Follow after love, and earnestly desire spiritual gifts, but especially that you may prophesy. For he who speaks in another language speaks not to men, but to God; for no one understands; but in the spirit he speaks mysteries. But he who prophesies speaks to men for their edification, exhortation, and consolation. He who speaks in another language edifies himself, but he who prophesies edifies the assembly. Now I desire to have you all speak with other languages, but rather that you would prophesy. For he is greater who prophesies than he who speaks with other languages, unless he interprets, that the assembly may be built up ... For if I pray in another language, my spirit prays, but my understanding is unfruitful.

— 1 Corinthians 14:1-5, 14 WEB

SECRETS OF THE HEART

But if all prophesy, and an unbeliever or an uninformed person comes in, he is convinced by all, he is convicted by all. And thus the secrets of his heart are revealed; and so, falling down on his face, he will worship God and report that God is truly among you ... Therefore, brethren, desire earnestly to prophesy, and do not forbid to speak with tongues. Let all things be done decently and in order.

— 1 Corinthians 14:24-25, 39-40 NKJV

EACH MEMBER BELONGS TO ALL THE OTHERS

For even as we have many members in one body, and all the members don't have the same function, so we, who are many, are one body in Christ, and individually members one of another. Having gifts differing according to the grace that was given to us, if prophecy, let us prophesy according to the proportion of our faith; or service, let us give ourselves to service; or he who teaches, to his teaching; or he who exhorts, to his exhorting: he who gives, let him do it with liberality; he who rules, with diligence; he who shows mercy, with cheerfulness.

— Romans 12:4-8 WEB

EACH ONE SHOULD USE HIS GIFT FAITHFULLY

The end of all things is near. Therefore be solemn and sober so you can pray. Above all things, have unfailing love for one another, because love covers a multitude of sins. Show hospitality to one another without complaining. As everyone has received a gift, even so serve one another with it, as good stewards of the manifold grace of God. If anyone speaks, let him speak as the oracles of God. If anyone serves, let him serve with the strength that God supplies, so that God in all things may be glorified through Jesus Christ, to whom be praise and dominion forever and ever. Amen.

— 1 Peter 4:7-11 MEV

THE PROMISE

And it shall come to pass afterward, that I will pour out my spirit upon all flesh; and your sons and your daughters shall prophesy, your old men shall dream dreams, your young men shall see visions: and also upon the servants and upon the handmaids in those days will I pour out my spirit.

— Joel 2:28-29 KJV

TESTIFY

I have previously shared that I was filled with the Holy Spirit in 1995. With study, I understood the need for spiritual gifts in my life. I was told a multitude of things by people in various denominations that brought confusion. So I will share my journey.

I understood the importance of having a prayer language that had not been released in me. I began to pursue this gift and periodically I would contend with the Lord for this gift for several months without success.

In 2011, through the course of events, I came to understand, by the revealing of the Holy Spirit, that my mind was being assaulted by torment. It was also revealed that I had been dealing with fear most of my life. It was only after being set free from torment and fear that my prayer language was released. Let me explain. A couple of months after being set free I began contending once again for my prayer language, and it was released like a dam had burst open.

I did not perceive the cause and effect between the oppression and the gift of tongues not being released but God is so faithful!!! I began seeking the Lord for the trigger or difference that allowed the release of this precious gift. About a month later while flipping through the television channels I stopped to listen to an older pastor that I did not recognize. Almost immediately he said something similar to this: If you have any demonic activity or influence in your life, it can block your Spiritual gifts. WOW! That was profound and brought great understanding to me. I am so very grateful.

Apply the possibility to yourself, looking deep for events or influences that have brought, or are bringing destruction to your life. Look carefully at the next verse.

Jesus speaking:

> The thief comes only in order to steal and kill and destroy. I came that they may have and enjoy life, and have it in abundance (to the full, till it overflows)

> — John 10:10 AMPC

PAUSE AND PONDER

DO YOU KNOW WHAT YOUR GIFTS ARE? ARE YOU USING THEM FOR THE GOOD OF THE BODY OF CHRIST?

If you are not sure of your gift or gifts ask the Lord and He will reveal it to you. Remember He often speaks in subtle promptings.

As everyone has received a gift, even so serve one another with it, as good stewards of the manifold grace of God.

— 1 Peter 4:10 MEV

A PRAYER YOU CAN PRAY

Verse 8 from the text below is one of my prayer verses.

"Father, I thank you for Holy Spirit and His gifts. Help me to use my gift for the body of Christ and His glory. Lord keep me strong to the end and help me to be blameless on the day of our Lord, Jesus Christ."

The Apostle Paul to the church in Corinth:

I thank my God always concerning you for the grace of God which was given to you by Christ Jesus, that you were enriched in everything by Him in all utterance and all knowledge, even as the testimony of Christ was confirmed in you, so that you come short in no gift, eagerly waiting for the revelation of our Lord Jesus Christ, who will also confirm you to the end, that you may be blameless in the day of our Lord Jesus Christ. God is faithful, by whom you were called into the fellowship of His Son, Jesus Christ our Lord.

— 1 Corinthians 1:4-9 NKJV

Lesson 16

Fruit Of The Holy Spirit

Lesson Highlight:

> *But the fruit of the Spirit is love, joy, peace, patience,*
> *kindness, goodness, faithfulness, gentleness, and self-*
> *control. Against such things there is no law. Those*
> *who belong to Christ have crucified the flesh with its*
> *passions and lusts. If we live by the Spirit, let's also*
> *walk by the Spirit. Let's not become conceited,*
> *provoking one another, and envying one another.*

— Galatians 5:22-26 WEB

Notice in the previous verse the word "fruit" and the verb "is" are both singular. So it seems our singular Spiritual fruit should be demonstrated in all these various ways. If you consider carefully the fruit of the Spirit and how difficult it would be to produce in your own strength it may be overwhelming. It is produced as you yield yourself to the leading of the Holy Spirit.

Fruit trees aren't concerned that they must produce fruit, it's what they do. It is their nature to produce fruit. Christians who are making an effort to draw closer to the Lord through prayer, study, and relationship with Jesus to grow into maturity WILL produce spiritual fruit. Little by little, baby step, by baby step we will look more like Him.

> O taste and see that the LORD is good: blessed is the man that trusteth in him.
>
> — Psalm 34:8 KJV

TESTIMONY

There is a person with whom I have had many negative encounters through the years. These encounters are unavoidable and almost always unpleasant. About ten years ago I had a dream. I was in a very large room with many people and this person was one of them.

Some of the people were sitting in chairs that were facing various directions but were positioned in an irregular circle. Others were milling about the room. The atmosphere was pleasant with people chatting and in various conversations.

I was sitting in the circle in a chair facing the center of the circle, and holding in my lap a beautiful serving tray with the most beautiful sliced fruit on it. I had to leave the room for a short period of time and placed the tray in my chair. As I returned to my seat I was very surprised to find much of my fruit had been eaten by two people. This person was one of those who had eaten my fruit. I feel the Lord was affirming and encouraging but also warning me to be careful what kind of spiritual fruit I produced. People are eating our fruit whether good, bad, or even rotten. We must be mindful of our fruit!!!

WATCH OUT!

> Beloved, don't believe every spirit, but test the spirits, whether they are of God, because many false prophets have gone out into the world.

— 1 John 4:1 WEB

For there will arise false Christs, and false prophets, and they will show great signs and wonders, so as to lead astray, if possible, even the elect.

— Matthew 24:24 WEB

Jesus speaking at the Sermon on the Mount:

Beware of false prophets, who come to you dressed as sheep, but inside they are devouring wolves. You will fully recognize them by their fruits. Do people pick grapes from thorns, or figs from thistles? Even so, every healthy (sound) tree bears good [fruit worthy of admiration], but the sickly (decaying, worthless) tree bears bad (worthless) fruit. A good (healthy) tree cannot bear bad (worthless) fruit, nor can a bad (diseased) tree bear excellent fruit [worthy of admiration]. Every tree that does not bear good fruit is cut down and cast into the fire. Therefore, you will fully know them by their fruits. Not everyone who says to Me, Lord, Lord, will enter the kingdom of heaven, but he who does the will of My Father Who is in heaven.

— Matthew 7:15-21 AMPC

THE TRUE VINE

Jesus said:

"I am the true vine, and My Father is the vinedresser. Every branch in Me that does not bear fruit He takes away; and every branch that bears fruit He prunes, that it may bear more fruit."

— John 15:1-2 NKJV

It is mature trees that bear fruit and pruning is an important part of caring for the fruit trees. God will cut away our dead and useless branches to increase growth and improve our fruit. It will be painful to our flesh, but if we work with Him to get rid of the bad it will facilitate the process. Otherwise, we may have to take another trip around the mountain to be pruned.

BEAR GOOD FRUIT

The fruit of the righteous is a tree of life. He who is wise wins souls.

— Proverbs 11:30 WEB

I, therefore, the prisoner of the Lord, exhort you to walk in a manner worthy of the calling with which you were called. With all humility, meekness, and patience, bearing with one another in love, be eager to keep the unity of the Spirit in the bond of peace.

— Ephesians 4:1-3 MEV

For once you were darkness, but now you are light in the Lord; walk as children of Light [lead the lives of those native-born to the Light]. For the fruit (the effect, the product) of the Light or the Spirit [consists] in every form of kindly goodness, uprightness of heart, and trueness of life. And try to learn [in your experience] what is pleasing to the Lord [let your lives be constant proofs of what is most acceptable to Him]. Take no part in and have no fellowship with the fruitless deeds and enterprises of darkness, but instead [let your lives be so in contrast as to] expose and reprove and convict them.

— Ephesians 5:8-11 AMPC

So, my brothers, you also have died to the law through the body of Christ, so that you may be married to another, to Him who has been raised from the dead, so that we may bear fruit for God. When we were in the flesh, the passions of sin, through the law, worked in our members to bear fruit leading to death. But now we are delivered from the law, having died to things in which we were bound, so that we may serve in newness of the Spirit, and not in the oldness of the letter of the law.

— Romans 7:4-6 MEV

Who also declared to us your love in the Spirit. For this cause, we also, since the day we heard this, don't cease praying and making requests for you, that you may be filled with the knowledge of his will in all spiritual wisdom and understanding, that you may walk worthily of the Lord, to please him in all respects, bearing fruit in every good work, and increasing in the knowledge of God

— Colossians 1:8-10 WEB

SOME THOUGHTS

As you ponder and consider your fruit, also give thought to how it holds up under pressure, trauma, or in a heated battle. Our fruit may be beautiful and tasty when all is going well but how much love, joy, peace, patience, kindness, goodness, faithfulness, gentleness and self-control will you be able to demonstrate when negative emotions are high and adversity present. We must be able to stand firm under pressure. Ask Holy Spirit to help you and He will.

Remember pruning and the Refiner's Fire is painful to our flesh. When they come, and they will, plant your feet and hang on. I made frequent trips to the bathroom at work, aka the prayer closet, grabbing the sink as though the horns of the altar and crying out to the Lord. My go-to prayer was this next verse:

Create in me a clean heart, O God; and renew a right spirit within me.

— Psalm 51:10 KJV

PAUSE AND PONDER

HAVE YOU COME TO UNDERSTAND THAT WE SHOULD PRODUCE MORE AND MORE OF THE FRUIT OF THE SPIRIT AS WE TRAVEL THE NARROW ROAD? HAVE YOU PERCEIVED THEY ARE THE VERY ATTRIBUTES OF GOD? HAVE YOU EMBRACED THEIR DEVELOPMENT IN YOUR LIFE?

For we were also once foolish, disobedient, deceived, serving various lusts and pleasures, living in malice and envy, hateful, and hating one another. But when the kindness of God, our Savior, and his love toward man, appeared, not by works of righteousness, which we did ourselves, but according to his mercy, he saved us, through the washing of regeneration and renewing by the Holy Spirit, which he poured out on us richly, through Jesus Christ, our Savior; that, being justified by his grace, we might be made heirs according to the hope of eternal life.

— Titus 3:3-7 WEB

A PRAYER YOU CAN PRAY

"Thank You Father for Your mercy, thank You for the Holy Spirit, and thank You for Jesus! Help me to embrace the pruning and to work with You to develop and maintain sweet, tasty fruit to draw others to You. In Jesus' name. Amen."

THE FOLLOWING VERSES ARE ABOUT THE FRUIT OF THE SPIRIT.

Some repetition of verses that cover more than one fruit.

> But the fruit of the Spirit is love, joy, peace, patience, kindness, goodness, faithfulness, gentleness, and self-control. Against such things there is no law. Those who belong to Christ have crucified the flesh with its passions and lusts. If we live by the Spirit, let's also walk by the Spirit. Let's not become conceited, provoking one another, and envying one another.
>
> — Galatians 5:22-26 WEB

LOVE

> We know and have believed the love which God has in us. God is love, and he who remains in love remains in God, and God remains in him. In this love has been made perfect with us, that we may have boldness in the day of judgment, because as he is, even so are we in this world.
>
> — 1 John 4:16-17 WEB

> If I speak with the languages of men and of angels, but don't have love, I have become sounding brass, or a clanging cymbal ... Love is patient and is kind; love doesn't envy. Love doesn't brag, is not proud, doesn't behave itself inappropriately, doesn't seek its own way, is not provoked, takes no account of evil; doesn't rejoice in unrighteousness, but rejoices with the truth; bears all things, believes all things, hopes all things, endures all things. Love never fails.
>
> — 1 Corinthians 13:1, 4-8a WEB

Above all things have intense and unfailing love for one another, for love covers a multitude of sins [forgives and disregards the offenses of others].

— 1 Peter 4:8 AMPC

JOY

I have spoken these things to you, that my joy may be in you, and that your joy may be made full.

— John 15:11 WEB

Then he said unto them, Go your way, eat the fat, and drink the sweet, and send portions unto them for whom nothing is prepared: for this day is holy unto our Lord: neither be ye sorry; for the joy of the LORD is your strength.

— Nehemiah 8:10 KJV

Yet I will rejoice in the LORD, I will joy in the God of my salvation.

— Habakkuk 3:18 KJV

PEACE

Jesus said:

Peace I leave with you, my peace I give unto you: not as the world giveth, give I unto you. Let not your heart be troubled, neither let it be afraid.

— John 14:27 KJV

Jesus said:

> These things I have spoken unto you, that in me ye might have peace. In the world ye shall have tribulation: but be of good cheer; I have overcome the world.

> — John 16:33 KJV

An "if/then" verse. If you do *this* then God will do *that*:

> Be careful for nothing; but in every thing by prayer and supplication with thanksgiving let your requests be made known unto God. And the peace of God, which passeth all understanding, shall keep your hearts and minds through Christ Jesus.

> — Philippians 4:6-7 KJV

PATIENCE

> However, for this reason I obtained mercy, that in me first Jesus Christ might show all longsuffering, as a pattern to those who are going to believe on Him for everlasting life.

> — 1 Timothy 1:16 NKJV

> Rejoicing in hope; patient in tribulation; continuing instant in prayer.

> — Romans 12:12 KJV

Rest in the LORD, and wait patiently for him: fret not thyself because of him who prospereth in his way, because of the man who bringeth wicked devices to pass.

— Psalm 37:7 KJV

KINDNESS

Let not mercy and kindness [shutting out all hatred and selfishness] and truth [shutting out all deliberate hypocrisy or falsehood] forsake you; bind them about your neck, write them upon the tablet of your heart.

— Proverbs 3:3 AMPC

Put on therefore, as God's elect, holy and beloved, a heart of compassion, kindness, lowliness, humility, and perseverance.

— Colossians 3:12 WEB

And beside this, giving all diligence, add to your faith virtue; and to virtue knowledge; and to knowledge temperance; and to temperance patience; and to patience godliness; and to godliness brotherly kindness; and to brotherly kindness charity. For if these things be in you, and abound, they make you that ye shall neither be barren nor unfruitful in the knowledge of our Lord Jesus Christ.

— 2 Peter 1:5-8 KJV

GOODNESS

Jesus said:

But love your enemies, and do good, and lend, expecting nothing back; and your reward will be great, and you will be sons of the Most High; for he is kind toward the unthankful and evil.

— Luke 6:35 WEB

Let us not be weary in doing good, for we will reap in due season, if we don't give up. So then, as we have opportunity, let us work that which is good toward all men, and especially toward those who are of the household of the faith.

— Galatians 6:9-10 WEB

But don't forget to be doing good and sharing, for with such sacrifices God is well pleased.

— Hebrews 13:16 WEB

GENTLENESS

But the wisdom that is from above is first pure, then peaceable, gentle, and easy to be entreated, full of mercy and good fruits, without partiality, and without hypocrisy.

— James 3:17 KJV

Therefore, as God's chosen people, holy and dearly loved, clothe yourselves with compassion, kindness, humility, gentleness and patience. Bear with each other and forgive one another if any of you has a grievance against someone. Forgive as the Lord forgave you.

— Colossians 3:12-13 NIV

Paul to Titus:

Remind them to be in subjection to rulers and to authorities, to be obedient, to be ready to every good work, to speak evil of no one, not to be contentious, to be gentle, showing all humility toward all men.

— Titus 3:1-2 WEB

FAITHFULNESS

The Good Samaritan was very faithful. Jesus speaking:

So he went to him and bandaged his wounds, pouring on oil and wine; and he set him on his own animal, brought him to an inn, and took care of him. On the next day, when he departed, he took out two denarii, gave them to the innkeeper, and said to him, 'Take care of him; and whatever more you spend, when I come again, I will repay you.'

— Luke 10:34-35 NKJV

Stand firm therefore in the liberty by which Christ has made us free, and don't be entangled again with a yoke of bondage.

— Galatians 5:1 WEB

Don't be afraid of the things which you are about to suffer. Behold, the devil is about to throw some of you into prison, that you may be tested; and you will have oppression for ten days. Be faithful to death, and I will give you the crown of life.

— Revelation 2:10 WEB

SELF-CONTROL

An overseer then must be blameless, the husband of one wife, sober, self-controlled, respectable, hospitable, able to teach; not given to drunkenness, not violent, not greedy for money, but patient, not argumentative, not covetous.

— 1 Timothy 3:2-3 MEV

But the end of all things is near. Therefore be of sound mind, self-controlled, and sober in prayer.

— 1 Peter 4:7 WEB

For the grace of God (His unmerited favor and blessing) has come forward (appeared) for the deliverance from sin and the eternal salvation for all mankind. It has trained us to reject and renounce all ungodliness (irreligion) and worldly (passionate) desires, to live discreet (temperate, self-controlled), upright, devout (spiritually whole) lives in this present world.

— Titus 2:11-12 AMPC

Lesson 17

God Cares For And Comforts You

Lesson Highlight:

Sing, O heavens; and be joyful, O earth; and break forth into singing, O mountains: for the LORD hath comforted his people, and will have mercy upon his afflicted.

— Isaiah 49:13 KJV

The Lord desires that none perish but all come to salvation (2 Peter 3:9). All include those in the bars, in the brothels, in the prisons, in the churches and every person to have ever lived. No amount of wickedness or sin that cannot be washed away from a truly repentant heart by the precious blood of Jesus Christ. The Word, the Bible, gives us instructions on how to live our lives according to His will and His way (2 Timothy 3:16). When we deviate from His instructions it brings sin into our lives that will bring destruction (Romans 6:16).

The decrees and commands set forth by God for us to follow are for our good (Deuteronomy 28:15). Sin brings death (Romans 6:23) and it separates us from our holy God (Isaiah 59:1-2). The Bible makes it very clear that if we love God we will obey Him (John 14:23). Obedience brings blessings (Luke 11:28). Get to it!

HE CARES FOR AND COMFORTS YOU

Cast all your care upon Him, because He cares for you.

— 1 Peter 5:7 MEV

Cast your burden on Yahweh, and he will sustain you. He will never allow the righteous to be moved.

— Psalm 55:22 WEB

Jesus speaking:

Come to Me, all you who labor and are heavy laden, and I will give you rest.

— Matthew 11:28 NKJV

Blessed be the God and Father of our Lord Jesus Christ, the Father of mercies and God of all comfort; who comforts us in all our affliction, that we may be able to comfort those who are in any affliction, through the comfort with which we ourselves are comforted by God.

— 2 Corinthians 1:3-4 WEB

HE WILL HELP YOU

"Call on Me in the day of trouble; I will deliver you, and you will glorify Me."

— Psalm 50:15 MEV

The Lord, He goes before you. He will be with you. He will not fail you nor forsake you. Do not fear, nor be dismayed.

— Deuteronomy 31:8 MEV

Don't you be afraid, for I am with you; don't be dismayed, for I am your God; I will strengthen you; yes, I will help you; yes, I will uphold you with the right hand of my righteousness ... For I, Yahweh your God, will hold your right hand, saying to you, Don't be afraid; I will help you.

— Isaiah 41:10, 13 WEB

The eyes of the Lord are on the righteous, And His ears are open to their cry ... The righteous cry out, and the Lord hears, And delivers them out of all their troubles. The Lord is near to those who have a broken heart, And saves such as have a contrite spirit. Many are the afflictions of the righteous, But the Lord delivers him out of them all.

— Psalm 34:15, 17-19 NKJV

And they laid their hands on the apostles, and put them in the common prison. But the angel of the Lord by night opened the prison doors, and brought them forth, and said, Go, stand and speak in the temple to the people all the words of this life.

— Acts 5:18-20 KJV

The angel said to him, "Put on your clothes, and tie on your sandals." He did so. He said to him, "Wrap your cloak around you, and follow me." He went out, and followed him. He didn't know that what was done by the angel was real, but thought he saw a vision. When they were past the first and the second guard, they came to the iron gate that leads into the city, which opened to them by itself. They went out, and passed on through one street, and immediately the angel departed from him. When Peter had come to himself, he said, "Now I truly know that the Lord has sent forth his angel and delivered me out of the hand of Herod, and from everything the Jewish people were expecting."

— Acts 12:8-11 WEB

GOD THE GOOD SHEPHERD, WE ARE HIS FLOCK

The LORD is my shepherd; I shall not want. He maketh me to lie down in green pastures: he leadeth me beside the still waters. He restoreth my soul: he leadeth me in the paths of righteousness for his name's sake. Yea, though I walk through the valley of the shadow of death, I will fear no evil: for thou art with me; thy rod and thy staff they comfort me.

— Psalm 23:1-4 KJV

Behold, the Lord GOD will come with strong hand, and his arm shall rule for him: behold, his reward is with him, and his work before him. He shall feed his flock like a shepherd: he shall gather the lambs with his arm, and carry them in his bosom, and shall gently lead those that are with young.

— Isaiah 40:10-11 KJV

So we, your people and sheep of your pasture, Will give you thanks forever. We will praise you forever, to all generations.

— Psalm 79:13 WEB

Jesus said to His disciples:

Fear not, little flock; for it is your Father's good pleasure to give you the kingdom.

— Luke 12:32 KJV

THE HOLY ONE, YOUR SAVIOR, IS WITH YOU ALWAYS

When you pass through waters, I will be with you. And through the rivers, they shall not overflow you. When you walk through the fire, you shall not be burned, nor shall the flame kindle on you, For I am the Lord your God, the Holy One of Israel, your Savior ...

— Isaiah 43:2-3a MEV

And the angel of God, which went before the camp of Israel, removed and went behind them; and the pillar of the cloud went from before their face, and stood behind them ... But the children of Israel walked upon dry land in the midst of the sea; and the waters were a wall unto them on their right hand, and on their left.

— Exodus 14:19, 29 KJV

And when those who bore the ark had come to the Jordan and the feet of the priests bearing the ark were in the brink of the water—for the Jordan overflows all its banks throughout the time of harvest— Then the waters which came down from above stood and rose up in a heap far off, at Adam, the city that is beside Zarethan; and those flowing down toward the Sea of the Arabah, the Salt [Dead] Sea, were wholly cut off. And the people passed over opposite Jericho. And while all Israel passed over on dry ground, the priests who bore the ark of the covenant of the Lord stood firm on dry ground in the midst of the Jordan, until all the nation finished passing over the Jordan.

— Joshua 3:15-17 AMPC

Then Nebuchadnezzar the king was astonished, and rose up in haste: he spoke and said to his counselors, Didn't we cast three men bound into the midst of the fire? They answered the king, True, O king. He answered, Look, I see four men loose, walking in the midst of the fire, and they have no hurt; and the aspect of the fourth is like a son of the gods. Then Nebuchadnezzar came near to the mouth of the burning fiery furnace: he spoke and said, Shadrach, Meshach, and Abed-nego, you servants of the Most High God, come forth, and come here. Then Shadrach, Meshach, and Abed-nego came forth out of the midst of the fire. The satraps, the deputies, and the governors, and the king's counselors, being gathered together, saw these men, that the fire had no power on their bodies, nor was the hair of their head singed, neither were their pants changed, nor had the smell of fire passed on them.

— Daniel 3:24-27 WEB

TESTIFY

God not only shows up for His sons and daughters but He meets us where we are. When I was a young woman I made a mistake and married a man with whom I was very unequally yoked. It developed into a bad situation and worsened as time went by. I went to church, helped to teach Sunday School, and paid tithes. I diligently prayed for the man to whom I was married to meet Jesus as Lord and Savior. When things got really bad and were unsafe my only choice was divorce.

I got angry at God. How very foolish and immature. I dug that hole myself and jumped in. I was in rebellion and disobedience when I married him. It was a terrible mistake that affected my daughter and I for a very long time. I was in my mid-twenties and did not have the understanding that God does not shove Himself down anyone's throat.

I thought if I prayed hard enough and long enough He would move on my ex-husband's heart. As I have reflected over the years I am certain that He did, although I could not perceive it through the very emotional circumstances at the time. I hope and pray he has received Jesus as his Lord and Savior.

Salvation is a choice that each person must make for themselves. Each individual has free will to choose or reject. There is no middle ground, saved or lost, sheep or a goat. You choose!!!

PAUSE & PONDER

ARE YOU DWELLING ON PAST MISTAKES AND FAILURES?

Heartfelt repentance and forgiveness are a must. You must forgive yourself and others. Ask for forgiveness from God and others as well. Then move forward and don't look back (Isaiah 43:18; Philippians 3:13; 2 Corinthians 5:17).

After you truly repent God forgives your sins and He forgets them.

As far as the east is from the west, so far hath he removed our transgressions from us.

— Psalm 103:12 KJV

I am the Lord, your Holy One, the creator of Israel, your King ... I, even I, am he that blotteth out thy transgressions for mine own sake, and will not remember thy sins.

— Isaiah 43:15, 25 KJV

Declares the Lord:

For I will be merciful to their unrighteousness, and their sins and their iniquities will I remember no more.

— Hebrews 8:12 KJV

A PRAYER YOU CAN PRAY

"Father, I repent for blaming You, please forgive me. Lord, forgive me for my past sins and failures. Lord bring people to my mind so that I may fully forgive them. Help me forgive myself and repent as I must. Help me to grasp the truth that once I repent and am forgiven these sins are gone in Your eyes and You never remember them again. They have been washed away. Thank You, Jesus!"

Lesson 18

Jesus Will Come Again

Lesson Highlight:

> *Don't marvel at this, for the hour comes, in which all that are in the tombs will hear his voice, and will come forth; those who have done good, to the resurrection of life; and those who have done evil, to the resurrection of judgment.*

> — John 5:28-29 WEB

The timing of His glorious return is one of great controversy and much debate. The Lord gave instructions on the many signs to watch for so that we will not be caught unaware of his return. He also cautioned us not to be deceived. Do not allow yourself to be snared nor troubled regarding this but rather fix your eyes on Jesus, the author and finisher of our faith (Psalm 25:15; Hebrews 2:10; Hebrews 12:2-3; Psalm 141:8).

JESUS WILL COME AGAIN

Jesus speaking to His disciples:

> But no one knows of that day and hour, not even the angels of heaven, but my Father only ... Therefore also be ready, for in an hour that you don't expect, the Son of Man will come.
>
> — Matthew 24:36, 44 WEB

As you read and reread these verses, ponder them for a while. Purpose in your heart to capture and retain those clues and signs of Jesus' return. Also, pay close attention to the warnings given to avoid deception.

WE ARE EXPECTANTLY WAITING

> As it is appointed for men to die once, but after this the judgment, so Christ was offered once to bear the sins of many. To those who eagerly wait for Him He will appear a second time, apart from sin, for salvation.
>
> — Hebrews 9:27-28 NKJV

> Looking for that blessed hope, and the glorious appearing of the great God and our Saviour Jesus Christ.
>
> — Titus 2:13 KJV

> But we are citizens of the state (commonwealth, homeland) which is in heaven, and from it also we earnestly and patiently await [the coming of] the Lord Jesus Christ (the Messiah) [as] Savior, Who will transform and fashion anew the body of our humiliation to conform to and be like the body of His glory and majesty, by

exerting that power which enables Him even to subject everything to Himself.

— Philippians 3:20-21 AMPC

Jesus speaking to His disciples at the Last Supper:

"Don't let your heart be troubled. Believe in God. Believe also in me. In my Father's house are many mansions. If it weren't so, I would have told you. I am going to prepare a place for you. If I go and prepare a place for you, I will come again, and will receive you to myself; that where I am, you may be there also."

— John 14:1-3 WEB

WATCH OUT THAT NO ONE DECEIVES YOU

Much of this chapter is about the end days:

As Jesus was sitting on the Mount of Olives, the disciples came to him privately. "Tell us," they said, "when will this happen, and what will be the sign of your coming and the end of the age?" Jesus answered: "Watch out that no one deceives you. For many will come in my name, claiming, 'I am the Messiah,' and will deceive many ... "If those days had not been cut short, no one would survive, but for the sake of the elect those days will be shortened." At that time if anyone says to you, 'Look, here is the Messiah!' or, 'There he is!' do not believe it. For false messiahs and false prophets will appear and perform great signs and wonders to deceive, if possible, even the elect. See, I have told you ahead of time. "So if anyone tells you, 'There he is, out in the wilderness,' do not go out; or, 'Here he is, in the inner rooms,' do not believe it. For as lightning that comes from the east is visible even in the west, so will be the coming of the Son of Man.

"Immediately after the distress of those days 'the sun will be darkened, and the moon will not give its light; the stars will fall from the sky, and the heavenly bodies will be shaken.' "Then will appear the sign of the Son of Man in heaven. And then all the peoples of the earth will mourn when they see the Son of Man coming on the clouds of heaven, with power and great glory. And he will send his angels with a loud trumpet call, and they will gather his elect from the four winds, from one end of the heavens to the other.

— Matthew 24:3-5, 22-27, 29-31 NIV

Now I urge you, brethren, note those who cause divisions and offenses, contrary to the doctrine which you learned, and avoid them. For those who are such do not serve our Lord Jesus Christ, but their own belly, and by smooth words and flattering speech deceive the hearts of the simple.

— Romans 16:17-18 NKJV

But evil men and impostors will grow worse and worse, deceiving and being deceived.

— 2 Timothy 3:13 WEB

Now, brothers, concerning the coming of our Lord Jesus Christ, and concerning our gathering together unto Him, we ask you not to let your mind be quickly shaken or be troubled, neither in spirit nor by word, nor by letter coming as though from us, as if the day of Christ is already here. Do not let anyone deceive you in any way. For that Day will not come unless a falling away comes first, and the man of sin is revealed, the son of destruction, who opposes and exalts himself above all that is called God or is worshipped, so that he sits as God in the temple of God, showing himself as God ... For the mystery of lawlessness is already working. Only He who is now restraining him will do so until he is taken out of the way. Then the lawless one will be revealed, whom the Lord will consume with the breath of His mouth, and destroy with the brightness of His presence.

— 2 Thessalonians 2:1-4, 7-8 MEV

SIGNS IN THE HEAVENS

Jesus replied to his disciples:

There shall be signs in the sun, and in the moon, and in the stars; and upon the earth distress of nations, with perplexity; the sea and the waves roaring; Men's hearts failing them for fear, and for looking after those things which are coming on the earth: for the powers of heaven shall be shaken. And then shall they see the Son of man coming in a cloud with power and great glory. And when these things begin to come to pass, then look up, and lift up your heads; for your redemption draweth nigh.

— Luke 21:25-28 KJV

Behold, the day of Yahweh comes, cruel, with wrath and fierce anger; to make the land a desolation, and to destroy the sinners of it out of it. For the stars of the sky and the constellations of it shall not give their light; the sun shall be darkened in its going forth, and the moon shall not cause its light to shine.

— Isaiah 13:9-10 WEB

Blow you the trumpet in Zion, And sound an alarm in my holy mountain! Let all the inhabitants of the land tremble, For the day of Yahweh comes, For it is close at hand: A day of darkness and gloominess, A day of clouds and thick darkness. As the dawn spreading on the mountains, A great and strong people; There has never been the like, Neither will there be any more after them, Even to the years of many generations ... The earth quakes before them. The heavens

tremble. The sun and the moon are darkened, And the stars withdraw their shining. Yahweh thunders his voice before his army; For
his forces are very great; For he is strong who obeys his command; For
the day of Yahweh is great and very awesome, And who can
endure it?

— Joel 2:1-2, 10-11 WEB

PEACE AND SAFETY

But concerning the times and the seasons, brothers, you have no need
that anything be written to you. For you yourselves know well that
the day of the Lord comes like a thief in the night. For when they are
saying, "Peace and safety," then sudden destruction will come on
them, like birth pains on a pregnant woman; and they will in no way
escape. But you, brothers, aren't in darkness, that the day should overtake you like a thief.

— 1 Thessalonians 5:1-4 WEB

FIRSTFRUITS

But now Christ has been raised from the dead. He became the first
fruits of those who are asleep. For since death came by man, the
resurrection of the dead also came by man. For as in Adam all die, so
also in Christ all will be made alive. But each in his own order: Christ
the first fruits, then those who are Christ's, at his coming.

— 1 Corinthians 15:20-23 WEB

That the Christ (the Anointed One) must suffer and that He, by
being the first to rise from the dead, would declare and show light
both to the [Jewish] people and to the Gentiles.

— Acts 26:23 AMPC

He is the head of the body, the church: who is the beginning, the first-born from the dead; that in all things he might have the preeminence.

— Colossians 1:18 KJV

THE TRUMPET WILL SOUND

Behold, I shew you a mystery; We shall not all sleep, but we shall all be changed, in a moment, in the twinkling of an eye, at the last trump: for the trumpet shall sound, and the dead shall be raised incorruptible, and we shall be changed.

— 1 Corinthians 15:51-52 KJV

THE COMING IN THE CLOUDS

But Jesus kept silent. And the high priest answered and said to Him, "I put You under oath by the living God: Tell us if You are the Christ, the Son of God!" Jesus said to him, "It is as you said. Nevertheless, I say to you, hereafter you will see the Son of Man sitting at the right hand of the Power, and coming on the clouds of heaven."

— Matthew 26:63-64 NKJV

For if we believe that Jesus died and rose again, even so them also which sleep in Jesus will God bring with him. For this we say unto you by the word of the Lord, that we which are alive and remain unto the coming of the Lord shall not prevent them which are asleep. For the Lord himself shall descend from heaven with a shout, with the voice of the archangel, and with the trump of God: and the dead in Christ shall rise first: Then we which are alive and remain shall be caught up together with them in the clouds, to meet the Lord in the air: and so shall we ever be with the Lord. Wherefore comfort one another with these words.

— 1 Thessalonians 4:14-18 KJV

Look! He is coming with clouds, and every eye will see Him, even those who pierced Him. And all the tribes of the earth will mourn because of Him. Even so, Amen.

— Revelation 1:7 MEV

SOON AND VERY SOON

Therefore don't throw away your boldness, which has a great reward. For you need patience, so that, having done the will of God, you may receive the promise. "For yet a very little while, He who comes will come, and will not wait. But the righteous will live by faith. If he shrinks back, my soul has no pleasure in him." But we are not of those who shrink back to destruction, but of those who have faith to the saving of the soul.

— Hebrews 10:35-39 WEB

I saw the heaven opened, and behold, a white horse, and he who sat on it is called Faithful and True. In righteousness he judges and makes war. His eyes are a flame of fire, and on his head are many crowns. He has names written and a name written which no one knows but he himself. He is clothed in a garment sprinkled with blood. His name is called "The Word of God." The armies which are in heaven followed him on white horses, clothed in white, pure, fine linen. Out of his mouth proceeds a sharp, two-edged sword, that with it he should strike the nations. He will rule them with a rod of iron. He treads the winepress of the fierceness of the wrath of God, the

Almighty. He has on his garment and on his thigh a name written, "KING OF KINGS, AND LORD OF LORDS."

— Revelation 19:11-16 WEB

"Behold, I come quickly. My reward is with me, to repay to each man according to his work. I am the Alpha and the Omega, the First and the Last, the Beginning and the End. Blessed are those who do his commandments, that they may have the right to the tree of life, and may enter in by the gates into the city. Outside are the dogs, the sorcerers, the sexually immoral, the murderers, the idolaters, and everyone who loves and practices falsehood. I, Jesus, have sent my angel to testify these things to you for the assemblies. I am the root and the offspring of David; the Bright and Morning Star."

— Revelation 22:12-16 WEB

Behold, I come quickly: blessed is he that keepeth the sayings of the prophecy of this book ... He which testifieth these things saith, Surely I come quickly. Amen. Even so, come, Lord Jesus.

— Revelation 22:7, 20 KJV

BE ABOUT OUR FATHER'S BUSINESS

Luke chapter 2:39-51 tells us that every year Mary and Joseph went to Jerusalem for the Feast of Passover. After Passover when Jesus was twelve years old, his parents and their group left for home but He stayed behind. After traveling for a day they realized He was not among the group and returned to Jerusalem to look for Him. Let's look at a few of these verses.

It happened after three days they found him in the temple, sitting in the midst of the teachers, both listening to them, and asking them questions. All who heard him were amazed at his understanding and his answers. When they saw him, they were astonished, and his mother said to him, "Son, why have you treated us this way? Behold, your father and I were anxiously looking for you."He said to them, "Why were you looking for me? Didn't you know that I must be in my Father's house?" They didn't understand the saying which he spoke to them.

— Luke 2:46-50 WEB

Verse 49 in the passage above in a different version:

And He said to them, How is it that you had to look for Me? Did you not see and know that it is necessary [as a duty] for Me to be in My Father's house and [occupied] about My Father's business?

— Luke 2:49 AMPC

We too must be about our Father's business:

Jesus came to them and spoke to them, saying, "All authority has been given to me in heaven and on earth. Go, and make disciples of all nations, baptizing them in the name of the Father and of the Son and of the Holy Spirit, teaching them to observe all things which I commanded you. Behold, I am with you always, even to the end of the age." Amen.

— Matthew 28:18-20 WEB

DO NOT GROW WEARY NOR LOSE HEART

We must not become fearful or anxious at the coming of the end but do what the Word instructs: "Keep your eyes fixed on Jesus!"

> Looking unto Jesus, the author and finisher of our faith, who for the joy that was set before Him endured the cross, despising the shame, and has sat down at the right hand of the throne of God. For consider Him who endured such hostility from sinners against Himself, lest you become weary and discouraged in your souls.
>
> — Hebrews 12:2-3 NKJV

Keep this next statement in the back of your mind, it will comfort you: **WE WIN!!!**

PAUSE AND PONDER

HAVE YOU CONSIDERED THAT YOU MAY SUFFER PERSE-CUTION BECAUSE OF JESUS? HAVE YOU DETERMINED IN YOUR HEART HOW YOU WILL RESPOND?

> If you are insulted for the name of Christ, blessed are you; because the Spirit of glory and of God rests on you. On their part he is blasphemed, but on your part he is glorified.
>
> — 1 Peter 4:14 WEB

We have been extremely blessed in the United States with little true persecution as in other nations around the world. I am very thankful. The day is coming when that will no longer be true, so determine in your heart ahead of time that you will not give up nor shrink back. "Be strong and courageous mighty warrior."

Jesus answered them, Be careful that no one misleads you [deceiving you and leading you into error] ... Then they will hand you over to suffer affliction and tribulation and put you to death, and you will be hated by all nations for My name's sake. And then many will be offended and repelled and will begin to distrust and desert [Him Whom they ought to trust and obey] and will stumble and fall away and betray one another and pursue one another with hatred. And many false prophets will rise up and deceive and lead many into error. And the love of the great body of people will grow cold because of the multiplied lawlessness and iniquity, But he who endures to the end will be saved. And this good news of the kingdom (the Gospel) will be preached throughout the whole world as a testimony to all the nations, and then will come the end.

— Matthew 24:4, 9-14 AMPC

There is only one chapter in Jude:

On some have compassion, making a distinction, and some save, snatching them out of the fire with fear, hating even the clothing stained by the flesh. Now to him who is able to keep them from stumbling, and to present you faultless before the presence of his glory in great joy, to God our Savior, who alone is wise, be glory and majesty, dominion and power, both now and forever. Amen.

— Jude 1:22-25 WEB

A PRAYER YOU CAN PRAY

"Lord, I ask You to help me to never shrink back or to be cowardly in confessing You as my Lord and Savior. Help me to be strong and courageous in Your precious holy name, Jesus. Amen." (Hebrews 10:37-38; 1 Corinthians 16:13; Matthew 10:32)

. . .

Then I heard a loud voice in heaven, saying: "Now the salvation and the power and the kingdom of our God and the authority of His Christ have come, for the accuser of our brothers, who accused them before our God day and night, has been cast down. They overcame him by the blood of the Lamb and by the word of their testimony, and they loved not their lives unto the death. Therefore rejoice, O heavens, and you who dwell in them! Woe unto the inhabitants of the earth and the sea! For the devil has come down to you in great wrath, because he knows that his time is short."

— Revelation 12:10-12 MEV

Reflection Questions

You may want to use a separate piece of paper for your answers.

Lesson 1 *God Is Big*

1. Who is The King over all the earth? (Psalm 47:2)
2. Can we hide from God's Presence? (Jeremiah 23:23-24)
3. Why did Jonah run away? (Jonah 1:3)
4. What did the Lord prepare for Jonah? (Jonah 1:17)

Lesson 2 *He Is All That You Need*

1. Find seven words that describe God. (Deuteronomy 32:4; Deuteronomy 7:9)
2. What are four things to do for God to rouse Himself on our behalf? (Job 8:5-7)
3. What must we do to find God? (Jeremiah 29:11-13)
4. What one word best describes God? (1 John 4:8)

Lesson 3 *He Is Unfathomable*

1. How old is God? (Job 36:26)
2. Regarding the stars, what does God do? (Psalm 147:4)
3. Who is the blessed and only _____, the ____of _____, and ____ of _____; (1 Timothy 6:15-16)
4. How does God speak? (Job 33:14)

Lesson 4 *The Trinity...Three Yet One*

1. Man was made in whose image? (Genesis 1:26)
2. How does the old hymn explain the Trinity? (Last line in each verse)
3. What is the name of the Word, the One and Only? (John 1:14, 18)
4. Who is the Comforter, Counselor, and Helper? (John 14:26)

Lesson 5 *God The Father*

1. From what did God form man when he was created? (Genesis 2:7)
2. He who doesn't love doesn't ____ ___, for God is love. (1 John 4:8)
3. The Lord has compassion on those who ____ ___; for He knows how we are formed, He remembers that we are dust. (Psalm 103:13)
4. How did the prodigal son's father react when he arrived home? (Luke 15:20)

Lesson 6 *The Ways Of God*

1. What did Moses ask of God? (Exodus 33:13)

2. Why did the Lord choose Abraham to be the father of His chosen people? (Genesis 18:19)
3. What three things did David ask of God? (Psalm 25:4-5)
4. What is the common thread in the three previous questions?

Lesson 7 *The Will, Purpose, And Plan Of God*

1. For the Son of man is come to....? Fill in the rest of the verse. (Luke 19:10)
2. What was the name Hagar, Sarai's servant, gave to Angel of the Lord?
3. In 1 Thessalonians 5:17 we are instructed to pray how?
4. What does 1 Corinthians 10:13 tell us about temptation? List three of these things.

Lesson 8 *God The Son, Jesus Christ*

1. How should we expect to see Jesus at His return? (Matthew 26:64)
2. Briefly discuss the gate by which we should enter. (Matthew 7:13-14; John 10:9)
3. Jesus is the image of the _____ ___. (Colossians 1:15)
4. In John 20:24-28 one of Jesus' disciples expressed great doubt about Jesus' return after the resurrection. What was his name?

Lesson 9 *The Ministry Of Jesus*

1. How can a person go to the Father? (John 14;6)
2. Look carefully at Psalm 18:2 and list each thing that the Lord is for His followers.
3. Colossians 1:15 says Jesus is the image of ___ _____ ___.

4. In the land of Cana Jesus performed the first sign of His ministry. What was the sign? At what event did this take place?

Lesson 10 *Our Messiah And Prophecies Foretold*

1. For no prophecy ever came by the will of man; but holy men of ___ _____, being moved by ___ ____ _____. (2 Peter 1:21)
2. Acts 2:29-32 KJV refers to King David as a prophet; it also shares the prophetic word he released. What was the word released?
3. Galatians 4:4-5 explains when the fullness of time was come something happened. What was it?
4. What were the last words spoken by Jesus on the cross? (John 19:30)

Lesson 11 *Christ Crucifixion*

1. When Jesus was reclining at the table with the Twelve, He revealed that one of them would _____ Him. (Matthew 26:20-22)
2. A man named _____ from _____ was forced to carry the cross of Christ to the Place of the Skull called, _____. (Matthew 27:32)
3. The written notice of the charge against Jesus was? (Mark 15:26)
4. Christ died for? (1 Peter 3:18)

Lesson 12 *Burial And Resurrection*

1. A rich man named _____ from _____ asked Pilate for Jesus' body. (Matthew 27:57)

2. In Acts 3:15 the Apostle Peter described Jesus how? (Acts 3:15)
3. Matthew 28:2 describes a violent earthquake as an angel came down from heaven. What did the angel do?
4. We must fix our eyes on Jesus, who is the ... ? (Hebrews 12:2)

Lesson 13 *God The Holy Spirit*

1. In Ezekiel 36:26 the Lord says He will remove...and give...
2. Jesus explained when the Spirit of truth comes he will guide us in ___ _____. (John 16:13)
3. When someone believes in Christ and receives salvation we are marked how? (Ephesians 1:13)
4. Sealed for ___ ___ of _____. (Ephesians 4:30)

Lesson 14 *Holy Spirit ... Our Helper*

1. In regards to the Holy Spirit, Ephesians 4:30 tells us ...
2. Also 1 Thessalonians 5:19 instructs us not to...
3. God poured ____ into our _____ by the Holy Spirit, whom he has given us. (Romans 5:5)
4. Jesus was, by the Holy Spirit, led into the desert to? (Matthew 4:1)

Lesson 15 *Gifts Of The Holy Spirit*

1. In Acts 2:38 Peter explains that after repenting, being baptized in the name of Jesus for forgiveness a person would receive the ____ of ____ _____.
2. List the spiritual gifts from 1 Corinthians 12:8-10.
3. Peter instructs us to be clear-minded and self-controlled so that...? (1 Peter 4:7)

4. ____ covers a multitude of ____. (1 Peter 4:8)

Lesson 16 *Fruit Of The Holy Spirit*

1. List the fruits of the Holy Spirit from Galatians 5:22-26.
2. Who is the true vine as revealed in John 15:1. Who is the gardener?
3. The gardener cuts away that ... ? (John 15:2)
4. In Galatians 5:24 it explains those who belong to Christ have crucified their _____ _____ with its _____ and _____.

Lesson 17 *God Cares For And Comforts You*

1. ____ your _____ on the Lord and he will sustain you ... (Psalm 55:22)
2. In Acts 5:18-20 how did God deliver the apostles after they were arrested?
3. God is our shepherd and we are His flock. List five things He does for us in Psalm 23?
4. How many men were tied and cast into the fiery furnace in Daniel 3:24-27? How many men did King Nebuchadnezzar see walking around in the fire unbound and unharmed?

Lesson 18 *Jesus Will Come Again*

1. What does Matthew say about the time of Jesus' return? (Matthew 24:36, 44)
2. What does Matthew 24 declare about the sun and the moon in verse 29?
3. It also speaks of the stars and the heavenly bodies. How does it describe them?

4. How will Jesus come when He returns? (Matthew 26:64; Revelation 1:7)

Bibliography

Lesson 6: The Ways Of God

"Way." Merriam-Webster.com Dictionary, Merriam-Webster, https://www.merriam-webster.com/dictionary/way. Accessed 13 Oct. 2021.

Lesson 8: God The Son, Jesus Christ

"Believe." Merriam-Webster.com Dictionary, Merriam-Webster, https://www.merriam-webster.com/dictionary/believe. Accessed 13 Oct. 2021.

"Faith." Merriam-Webster.com Dictionary, Merriam-Webster, https://www.merriam-webster.com/dictionary/faith. Accessed 13 Oct. 2021.

"Doubt." Merriam-Webster.com Dictionary, Merriam-Webster, https://www.merriam-webster.com/dictionary/doubt. Accessed 13 Oct. 2021.

Lesson 9: The Ministry Of Jesus

"Savior." Merriam-Webster.com Dictionary, Merriam-Webster, https://www.merriam-webster.com/dictionary/savior. Accessed 13 Oct. 2021.

Lesson 10: Our Messiah And The Prophecies Foretold

"Prophecy." Merriam-Webster.com Dictionary, Merriam-Webster, https://www.merriam-webster.com/dictionary/prophecy. Accessed 13 Oct. 2021.

Lesson 15: Gifts Of The Holy Spirit

"Gift." Merriam-Webster.com Dictionary, Merriam-Webster, https://www.merriam-webster.com/dictionary/gift. Accessed 13 Oct. 2021.

About the Author

Donna Ladner Bass by profession a Registered Nurse, by passion a seeker of God, who when unable to find just the right book to give to new believers composed *Big God, Getting To Know Him*. Beginning her career in 1986 it did not take long for her to realize the harvest field was ripe by way of the medical field. When people with their families and significant others in tow presented for medical help there was great pain, need, or distress that was their motivation. As a result of the needs and pain of those encountered Donna developed a strong practice of Intercessory prayer and sharing the good news of the Gospel through word, books, Bibles, pamphlets, and salvation cards.

She is married with two children and five grandchildren. In 2013 she found it necessary due to changes in family needs and responsibilities to end her employment. This true blessing in disguise also made it possible for the increase of time spent in prayer and Bible study. It allowed for deep roots to develop with much spiritual growth in her relationship with her Lord and Savior Jesus Christ.

Donna's intended goal for this series is to assist the reader in setting foundational truths by making key verses readily available. Establishing these truths is key and necessary for believers to more effectively navigate the narrow. It is her hope and desire that you enjoy and also anticipate more, yet to come.

Other Books by

3 TREES
PUBLISHING

A Publishing Assist Company

Honor & Excellence as the Seedbed of Your Written Work

3 Trees Publishing was born the result of an architectural buildout of Wells of SouthGate. 3 Trees Publishing serves to reconnect creatives with their kingdom calling by supplying a framework of excellence for all printed work.

Let the expression of your purpose be revealed as you prepare your legacy in print.

For more information, contact 3Treespublishing@gmail.com

The Destiny Series Books

STRATEGIC TRAINING TO DISCOVER YOU

The Destiny Series is designed to help you discover the who and the why that you are. You are designed to become a great leader that God intended you to be, and you can reach your maximum potential in the ministry that the Lord Jesus gave every person (Matthew 28:19).

This dynamic and interactive series is available for individual or group study, as well as an author led course. To learn more, use QR code to view books now available by Author, Rebecca D. Bennett and much more.

3Trees Publishing

His sound reverberates. Can you hear Him speak your name?

The Name Speaks by author Angela Broussard is an introduction to the Master Poet and His creation: *you*. Engage in the formation of your identity within the context of the Kingdom of God. Come into the knowledge of your vital role of service to the King, displayed within your given name.

Meet the Architect of Oikos: the Creator-King who fashioned seven pillars of wisdom to sustain Kingdom culture: marriage, family, maturing sons & daughters, stewardship, kingdom economy and creative commerce, authority, and worship. Against the backdrop of Matthew 19, Jesus' encounter with the rich young ruler provides an examination point of current cultural practices. The text exposes the pillars of Kingdom culture in such a way that the reader is able to inspect their arena of influence for structural breach. *Will you embrace cultural stability to promote growth and maturity? Will you be counted as a reformer?*

The Architect of Oikos & the Blueprints of Kingdom Culture is the second installment of the Doors Gates & Thresholds Series by author Angela Broussard.

God is calling, will you answer?

A Royal Disgrace: I Fell - Now What? Author Dwayne Jacobs exhorts every person plagued by the past: you can find restoration as a son in the Kingdom of God! The gifts and callings of God are without repentance. He does not withdraw what He has given, nor does He change His mind about those to whom He sent His call. This book is about the love of God that draws men to repentance, that times of refreshing may come.

* * *

Prophetic Expressions of His Love: 31 Days of Devotion Face to Face with the Spirit of God is a personal invitation from the Heavenly Father calling you to the secret place, to an encounter in His presence, where discovery of a love beyond comprehension begins as you are tuned to the sound of His heartbeat. Here you come to know Him and are known by Him; Beloved, it's time for you to know who you  are and what your true purpose is. Each day is a new way to see what the Father sees and to believe what He says. Dare to believe Him with all of your heart and you will see miracles happen all around you. Author Paula Jacobs

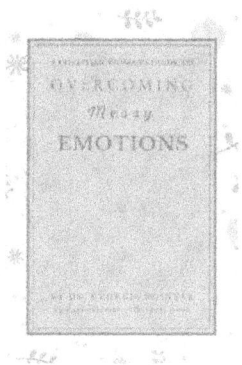

As a follower of Christ, you want your life to reflect His love and grace, but your emotions do not cooperate. With thought-provoking questions to help you get to the heart of your issues and the space provided to process your thoughts, *A Christian Woman's Guide to Overcoming Messy Emotions* is a valuable tool. Give yourself (or someone you care about) the gift of biblical truth that equips you to overcome! Author Georgia Pointer

* * *

Big God, Getting To Know Him: A New Believer's Guide To God by Donna L. Bass How big is God? He is BIG! Yet, He is not hidden, or hard to get to know. His ways are available to understand and experience. This set of self-guided lessons are your introduction to God in a BIG way! Inside are foundational truths that will help you journey into an ever increasing relationship with a BIG God. Be a learner and follower of God's ways and discover how BIG His purpose is for you!

Upcoming Titles 2024:

The Barley Company by Angela Broussard
You Can Live Again by Karla Tyrpak
Think On These Things by Georgia Pointer

Education

Kingdom Leadership Institute Gulf Coast

KLI GULF COAST

The leadership institute of choice prepares you for leadership in the Kingdom of God. The strategy of Kingdom Leadership Institute Gulf Coast is individualized. Your leadership training can begin at any level of spiritual and ministry maturity. We start where you are with what you do.

As one can function in any aspect of culture, once taught to function in kingdom culture, the Institute educates and prepares students for any arena of occupation. We honor kingdom leaders from every walk of life. Students come from many professions and occupations.

Partnered with KLI Jacksonville, our course intensives develop mature individuals to impact the current culture with Kingdom culture. Determine today to engage your life's work at the starting gate of Kingdom Leadership Institute Gulf Coast. For more information or to enroll, please use QR code or contact us via email at kligulfcoast@gmail.com.

Wells
of SouthGate

....

Serve, Train, Empower

We Bring the Trainer to You.

- Community Advancement
- Business Training
- Leadership Development

Wells of SouthGate is a training, equipping, and activating center on the Mississippi Gulf Coast.

Our passion is to see each person matured to fulfill our God-given dreams and destiny, to become a flourishing, contributing member of their society. For more information, use QR code to visit the Wells of SouthGate website.

www.ingramcontent.com/pod-product-compliance
Lightning Source LLC
Chambersburg PA
CBHW071157130626
46553CB00004B/1690